THE BATTLE OF ALLATOONA PASS

THE BATTLE OF ALLATOONA PASS

Civil War Skirmish in Bartow County, Georgia

BRAD BUTKOVICH

Charleston London

THE
History
PRESS

Published by The History Press
Charleston, SC 29403
www.historypress.net

Copyright © 2014 by Brad Butkovich
All rights reserved

Cover image: *The Battle of Allatoona Pass* by Don Troiani.

First published 2014

Manufactured in the United States

ISBN 978.1.62619.461.8

Library of Congress CIP data applied for.

To Anya, Lexi and Jack. You are my inspiration.

Contents

CONTENTS

Preface

Not only does a historian have to get the facts straight, but he or she also has to decide how to present those facts to the reader. This can be a daunting task, and each author tackles the effort differently. I think it is helpful to readers to explain how and why some of the information in the book is presented the way it is. How things read in a narrative is an organic element of the story and influences how the information is perceived by the reader.

The United States military—like most militaries throughout time, for that matter—is a very organized institution, as was its Confederate counterpart. It loved naming things and, in fact, required individual designations for objects and units. Logistics are the key to victory. Only the generals and politicians who can get the food and ammunition to the front lines will win, regardless of the tactical acumen of their field leaders. In order to do so, everything must have a name and a place. This holds true for the military units themselves. Those involved at Allatoona Pass have similar and confusing names, so it's worth a few moments to explain the differences between them.

The most important difference is the armies of the two combatants. The Confederate units at the battle were part of an army called the Army of Tennessee. On the other hand, the Federals were part of the Army of *the* Tennessee. Smaller units—such as corps, divisions and brigades—either were given a numerical designation, in the case of the Union, or were named after their commander, in the case of the Confederacy. So, for example, a

Union corps would be known as the Fifteenth Corps, while a Confederate one was known as Stewart's Corps. I prefer to write out the numerical designations for Union corps, as opposed to the popular use of Roman numerals. The participants themselves did so in their own writings, and I think it flows better and looks more natural in prose. Confederate units were proper names, so both the name of the leader and the unit—be it corps, division or brigade—are capitalized. Federal units, if referred to by their commanding officer, are not. Regiments on both sides were given numerical designations based on the state from which they were raised. So, on one hand, you would have the 4th Minnesota fighting for the North, and the 29th North Carolina for the South. Often you could encounter regiments from the border states fighting on opposite sides, such as Missouri or Kentucky, but thankfully, this did not occur at Allatoona. Unless otherwise noted, all the units that fought at Allatoona did so as infantry. There were ex-cavalry units present, such as the 10th Texas Cavalry (dismounted) and the 1st and 3rd Missouri Cavalry. However, they had turned in their horses years before and fought dismounted as infantry. They are referred to as simply the 1st and 3rd Missouri in the text, with their proper designation in the Order of Battle.

Several place names have changed in the intervening 150 years. Big Shanty is now the city of Kennesaw, while what was once Kennesaw Station is now merely a neighborhood outside the current Kennesaw battlefield park. In all cases, I have used the historical names that were in use in 1864. I used similar convention with quotes from the participants. Direct quotes are presented in the text exactly as the original author wrote them, errors and all, without the conventional "[sic]." I find the use of "[sic]" to be jarring, and showing how the original author wrote adds flavor and character to the prose. The Order of Battle provides a breakdown of the units that fought the battle, as well as their strengths and casualties if available. Hopefully this book will provide a comprehensive overview of the battle and lead to a more thorough understanding of the events leading up to and occurring on that memorable day.

Another fascinating and often overlooked facet of the battle at Allatoona is the campaign that preceded it. Most histories of the battle only mention in passing the details of the march leading up to the battle. Hood crosses the Chattahoochee, Sherman follows, the Confederates tear up the Western & Atlantic Railroad and then the Confederates arrive at the pass. I believe that there is a wealth of information that has been left out of print because of this oversight. The Confederate supply chain was in deplorable condition, and Sherman almost started his pursuit from Atlanta too late to affect the outcome of the battle. The Union garrisons along the railroad led a less than safe existence, and they also put up a much more spirited fight for their posts than previously recorded. All of these details deserve to be written and preserved for history.

Acknowledgements

This book, my second, gave me the opportunity to reach out and call on a variety of sources. The Battle of Allatoona was a relatively small affair, and this cries out for individual anecdotes and personal sources such as letters and diaries. I had the fortune of establishing contact with quite a few individuals who were able to provide me with previously unpublished material. For that, I am grateful.

First, I would like to thank the staff of the Atlanta History Center. They were extremely helpful and understanding to a first-time researcher such as myself. They patiently waited and pulled practically every map, photograph and journal in the collection of noted Atlanta historian/artist Wilbur Kurtz Sr. I'm sure it was tedious, but the research was immensely helpful to me and laid the groundwork for several future projects.

The 7th Illinois Infantry and its Henry repeating rifles played prominent roles in the battle. Historians as well as readers are drawn to the unique and the different. The thought of a Civil War battle fought with "modern" weapons such as the Henry and the Spencer family of firearms has caught the public's imagination for decades. With the help of Andrew L. Bresnan of the National Henry Rifle Company, I was able track down several primary sources detailing the actions of the 7th on that fateful October day. He also pointed me to the Abraham Lincoln Presidential Library in Springfield, Illinois. Reference librarian Gwen Podeschi helped me by tracking down and copying pages out of the large and unwieldy bound collection of annual reunion programs for the regiment's veterans. Her help was instrumental in discovering how the regiment came to possess the Henrys, along with other helpful anecdotes.

I would also like to thank Susan Fernie, great-granddaughter of Colonel William H. Clark of the 46th Mississippi Infantry. With only one line in his commanding officer's report describing Clark's death, it was assumed that he died relatively instantly on the battlefield. Two letters in Ms. Fernie's possession, written by an enlisted member of the regiment, provide a different account and bring to life Colonel Clark's devotion to his wife.

The Confederate artillery present at the battle has been something of a mystery. R. Jackson Rogers Sr., author of an upcoming book on the Pointe Coupée Artillery titled *The Splendid Pointe Coupee Artillery*, helped me determine the composition of the three-battery artillery battalion that marched with the Confederates into battle. Records on the artillery and their crews are scarce, but Rogers provided me with an excerpt from battery member Caesar Landry's diary that provided very useful information. My thanks for being a sounding board and helping to work through the activities of several Confederate artillery batteries in the days and weeks prior to the battle.

I'd also like to thank Dr. Steven Davis, author of *What the Yankees Did to Us: Sherman's Bombardment and Wrecking of Atlanta*, for agreeing to read over my finished manuscript and give me advice on any errors, as well as overall feedback. I hope I can return the favor one day.

Finally, of course, I have to thank my wife, Holley, and our three children for having patience and understanding as their daddy took day trips to various battlefields, libraries and archives. Without their continued support, I would never have been able to finish this book. I am forever indebted to my wife for the love and assistance she has given me throughout my crazy attempts at writing and studying history.

Introduction

The Battle of Allatoona Pass is a largely forgotten and overlooked battle. Sandwiched between the fall of Atlanta and the beginning of John Bell Hood's invasion of Tennessee, the fight gets a cursory mention in histories. There are few books dedicated solely to the struggle along the Western & Atlantic Railroad that fateful October morning. The memory of the men and women who fought there deserve better. The battle produced casualty rates that equaled or exceeded the most famous battles of the war, with far fewer men engaged. The result was an intense, sharp fight that left a much larger percentage of the soldiers actually engaged mangled and dead on the field.

The outcome effectively thwarted Hood's attempt to inflict any serious or long-lasting damage to the railroad, the lifeline of supplies for William T. Sherman's Union armies occupying Atlanta. He would continue to break the track and capture garrisons along its route, but with Sherman's armies caught up and in hot pursuit, Hood would never again have an opportunity to damage the railroad in any manner that could not be repaired in a few weeks' time. Modern full-length studies of the battle have only begun to be published in the last two decades, and yet none has thoroughly detailed the battle from the perspective of the men who did the fighting and dying in the forts and trenches surrounding the garrison. This book is an attempt to bring the stories of these soldiers to light in an informative and, above all, entertaining manner.

For such a small battle, there is plenty of material available and no shortage of controversies. Did the Union commander at Allatoona, John

M. Corse, ignore the Confederates' ultimatum to surrender, or did his reply simply fail to arrive in time? Why did the Confederate commander at the scene, Samuel G. French, call off the battle with victory within his grasp? The U.S. Signal Corps played a vital role in the battle, but there has been much confusion about what messages were sent and when. Did they inspire the men during the battle itself, or was it a postwar fabrication fed by a popular hymn? Who is the unknown Confederate soldier who was buried next to the tracks shortly after the battle and whose grave can still be visited today? When you add to these questions other fascinating aspects of the battle, such as the prevalent use of repeating rifles and brave men crossing a narrow footbridge over a deep chasm to get ammunition, you have the recipe for a captivating story indeed.

In addition to the men who fired the rifles and manned the cannons, the units they formed had unique histories and even personalities of their own. Their experiences, victories and defeats were often an accurate measure of how they would perform in combat, and the fight at Allatoona was no exception. Their history is an integral part of the story, as is the ground over which they fought. Maps are an essential part of any battle history, and this book is no exception. A heavy emphasis is placed on campaign and tactical maps to help the reader understand the nature and flow of the battle.

In the end, however, the outcome at Allatoona rested on the shoulders of the brave, scared and ultimately fallible officers, men and, yes, women who fought along the ridge that morning. Their actions deserve to be told and in detail. Some would rise to the occasion and be forever remembered by their comrades in word and in print. Others would succumb to their fear and be used, quite literally, as footstools. This is their story.

Chapter 1

To Fill Their Ranks

After hours of enduring relentless sun, choking smoke and quenchless thirst, the soldiers in the lonely fort atop the hill did not realize, at first, that the battle had ended. The sporadic gunfire from the enemy outside suddenly stopped. Nobody wanted to be the first to invite a lead ball to the forehead, so several cautious soldiers removed their hats, placed them on the end of their rifle's ramrods and slowly raised them above the walls of the fort. When nothing happened, furtive glances above the parapet replaced the hats. None drew enemy fire. With a rush of adrenaline, first one man and then half a dozen leapt over the walls. The fearless were quickly followed by the willing, and soon scores of men were filing out of the fort into open ground. Ignoring the carnage before them, order replaced chaos, and the officers hastily assembled scouts and skirmishers to pursue the enemy down the road they had taken. When they reached the first crossroads, they spied their quarry, more than two hundred yards distant, marching away and disappearing from sight.[1]

Emotions subdued and held in check during combat burst forth like an open floodgate. Cries of triumph and victory tore from the throats of the Union men and reverberated among the nearby hills. Soldiers shook hands and embraced one another with unabashed affection. Then came the tears. Tears of joy, tears of exhaustion and tears of anguish, for the living were not alone among the triumphant.[2]

Lieutenant William Ludlow emerged from the fort to confront a ghastly sight. The ditch surrounding the fortification had been used as an ad hoc trench by the defenders, and it was filled with a carpet of dead and wounded men. The injured writhed and struggled in their agony to remove themselves, while the dead continued their vigil. The survivors came to find and assist their wounded comrades, and soon every house and building in the surrounding community was filled to capacity. Casualties stretched far beyond the immediate garrison, and Ludlow toured the devastation. Following a ridge down from the fort, he retraced his steps from that morning. He passed a house and a ravine where his Confederate opponents had assembled for their final attacks. Cannon fire from the fort had torn them to shreds, as did the firepower of their new repeating rifles. Their mangled and upturned bodies gave mute testimony to the power of man's latest weapons of war.

Still, the sight that appalled Ludlow the most was the scene at the outer redoubt, or small fort, just beyond the house. The main struggle for the garrison had begun there earlier that morning. He found it difficult to stand before the carnage without a rush of tears, and a spasm of pity clutched at his throat. The men in the outpost had been ordered to hold it to the last, and earthworks were filled with bodies in blue and butternut uniforms. Bayonets and rifle butts had been used freely, and many of the dead remained locked together in their final embrace. The defenders had endeavored to fulfill their order to hold, as Ludlow would write decades later, with supreme fidelity.[3]

As the lieutenant surveyed the aftermath of the battle, a surgeon joined him and invited him to one of the makeshift hospitals. As they walked, the man surprised Ludlow with an unexpected detail: among the wounded soldiers was a woman in Confederate uniform. The lieutenant was taken aback, and the surgeon asked him to try and pick her out from among her comrades. As they made their way among the wounded, Ludlow confessed that he saw no woman. The doctor stopped at a bed on which lay a young soldier, tanned and freckled, leaning on one elbow and smoking a corncob pipe.

"How do you feel?" asked the doctor.

"Pretty well," the young soldier replied, "but my leg hurts like the devil."

"That is the woman," the doctor said as he turned to Ludlow. He explained that she was a member of the Missouri brigade they had just fought. She had followed her husband and one or two brothers to fight off the invaders. When they were killed earlier in the war, having no other home but their regiment, she took up a musket and joined the ranks. Now she would lose a leg for the cause.[4]

What a cause it must have been, too, that enlisted young women to stand shoulder to shoulder with a generation willing to sacrifice all for what they believed. On a bright October day in 1864, the consequences of that cause played out in a most violent manner among the hills and trenches of a small outpost named Allatoona Pass.

Chapter 2

Three Cheers for Joe Johnston!

G eneral John Bell Hood was a failure as an army commander, at least so far, and he would have to work hard to keep his job. Atlanta had fallen. Preventing the city from falling into Union hands could have denied Abraham Lincoln the military victory he needed to remain in office in the upcoming November presidential election. Unfortunately, Hood was at the helm of the Confederate army responsible for its defense and proved unable to stop the massive Union armies commanded by Major General William Tecumseh Sherman from capturing the city on September 2. Morale was low, desertions were up and Hood had to come up with a plan to reverse his fortune, and the Confederacy's as well.[5]

The progress of the rebellion looked grim. The year 1864 had been a brutal one, characterized by marginal victories, lost territory and, above all, massive casualties. In Virginia, the spring and summer campaign had been marked by a series of battles between Confederate general Robert E. Lee and his Union opponent, Lieutenant General Ulysses S. Grant. These battles ended in a deadlock before the city of Petersburg and the capital of Richmond. Confederate successes along the Red River in Louisiana and a momentary threatening of the Union capital had done little to reverse the overall course of the war. The fall of Atlanta after a four-month campaign had been a devastating blow. With the war in Virginia stalled, all eyes were on the adversaries in Georgia to make the next move.

Hood had a number of issues to resolve. First, he had to decide on the next course of action for his Army of Tennessee. Originally at Lovejoy Station after the fall of the city, Hood moved the army north to Jonesborough, site of the final battle of the campaign, on September 8. On the eighteenth, he shifted the army west to the small town of Palmetto, southwest of Atlanta, with the right of the line touching the West Point Railroad and the left resting on the Chattahoochee River. From there, he could wait to see what Sherman in Atlanta would do. Alternately, he could take the initiative and act first. It wasn't in Hood's nature to wait, and if he had learned anything from his former commander, Lee, it was that maintaining the initiative was paramount to success.

The question then became one of objectives. Attacking Sherman directly in Atlanta was out of the question, as the Union armies there outnumbered his and were ensconced behind the very earthworks Hood had occupied less than a month before. Transferring the army to another theater of the war was politically unfeasible, as it would invite Sherman to march unopposed through the nation's heartland to either Mobile or Savannah. Hood set his mind on the one remaining option: to move the Army of Tennessee north of Atlanta, destroy Sherman's railroad supply line between Atlanta and Chattanooga and force the Federals to attack him on his terms. If Sherman declined battle and moved toward the coast instead, Hood could attack him from behind, deny him supplies and forage for his men and defeat him in isolation. Hood had advocated taking the offensive as early as the sixth, shortly after abandoning Atlanta, and he telegraphed his latest plan to the authorities in Richmond on the twenty-first.[6]

That same evening, Hood learned that Confederate president Jefferson Davis had accepted an earlier invitation to visit the army and was on his way. Presidential visits to the Army of Tennessee by Davis were nothing new, and they were not always viewed in a positive light. In the opinion of one Texan, a visit from Davis portended disaster. The president had consulted with General Braxton Bragg before the defeat at Stone's River in 1862, visited the army to quell a near mutiny among the senior leadership before the rout at Chattanooga in 1863 and was now on the way to personally evaluate the situation and decide on the best course of action. "Now after all that experience, he comes here just after the fall of Atlanta to concoct some other plan for our defeat and display of his Generalship," lamented the Texan.[7]

Strategic decisions weren't the only ones on the table. Several prominent politicians were clamoring for Hood's removal after the loss of Atlanta, and it was an issue that Davis couldn't ignore. He would have to make a decision whether to keep Hood or replace him. If he replaced Hood, who could he find to fill the position? In addition, personnel conflicts were again sapping the proficiency of the army's high command. Hood placed much of the blame for the loss of Atlanta on the shoulders of his senior corps commander, Lieutenant General William J. Hardee. Something had to be done to salvage whatever harmony remained in the army's high command, not to mention the morale of the army itself.[8]

Davis arrived in Palmetto on the twenty-fifth, accompanied by two aides-de-camp. He and Hood immediately set to work crafting a workable plan of action. The commanding general laid out his plan in detail: move on Sherman's supply line, bring him to a decisive battle on the Confederates' terms if he marches to oppose Hood or pursue and isolate Sherman if he marches for the coast. Davis was in general agreement. Hood later wrote that he also put forth the contingency of invading Tennessee if practicable, but Davis later denied it in his own postwar writings. Regardless, the plan to cross north of the Chattahoochee and strike the railroad was agreed to in principle.[9]

The next day, Hood, Davis and their staffs rode out to the works and made an informal tour of the army. The result was more than a little embarrassing for the two on at least one occasion. While riding the lines and reviewing the men in Stewart's Corps, Colonel William H. Clark of the 46th Mississippi cried out in his thin voice, "Three cheers for President Davis and Gen. Hood!" Raising his sword aloft, he raised a yell, but it was only answered feebly by one or two others. Then, somebody else in the ranks shouted, "Three cheers for Gen. Joe Johnston!" the officer Davis had replaced with Hood in the middle of the Atlanta Campaign. This was responded to enthusiastically, and soon the entire brigade was yelling. The chagrin of the two men was palpable, and even Hood was forced to acknowledge it, or another similar incident, in his memoirs. The feeling was not universal. That evening, the president was serenaded by the band of the 20th Louisiana, and afterward, the men called on him to make a speech. He gave a short, spirited oration that called for a return to middle Tennessee and was heartily received by those present. The speech was followed by several others, including ones from Hood, General Howell Cobb and displaced Tennessee governor Isham G. Harris.[10]

The president spent the next day, the twenty-seventh, conferring with the remaining senior leadership of the Army of Tennessee. He first met with corps commanders Lieutenant General Alexander P. Stewart and Lieutenant General Stephen D. Lee in a house not far from Hood's tent. Afterward, he held a private meeting alone with General Hardee. Later in the evening, close to 6:00 p.m., Davis and his retinue mounted

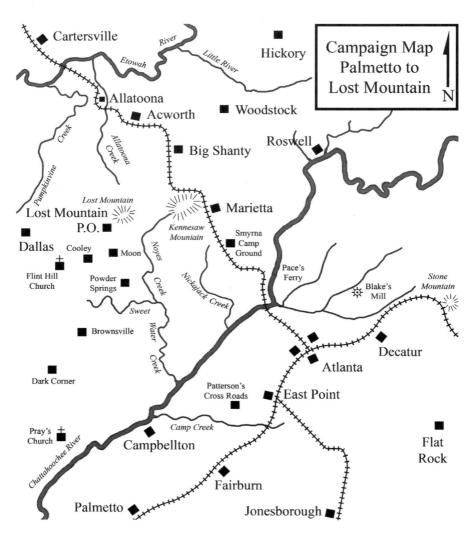

Campaign map from Jonesborough to Cartersville. *Courtesy of the author.*

their horses for the return ride to the railroad station. He was playing his hand close to his chest and had not announced a final decision to anyone. As Hood remembered it, Davis remarked that "he might find it necessary to assign another to the command of the Army, but I should continue to pursue my proposed plan, at least till a decision was reached in the matter." With that, Davis left, boarded the train and proceeded to Montgomery, Alabama.[11]

The wait was not a long one. The next day, Hood received the following telegram:

> *Relieve Lieutenant-General Hardee from duty with the Army of Tennessee, and direct him to proceed at once to Charleston, S.C., and assume command of the Department of South Carolina, Georgia, and Florida.*

Later, he received an additional telegram:

> *GENERAL: I have anxiously reflected upon the subject of our closing conversation, and the proposition confidentially mentioned. It seems to me best that I should confer with General Beauregard, and if quite acceptable to him, to place him in command of the department, embracing your army and that of General R. Taylor, so as to secure the fullest co-operation of the troops, without relieving either of you of the responsibilities and powers of your special commands, except so far as would be due to the superior rank and the above assignment of General Beauregard. He would necessarily, if present with either army, command in person. Before final action there will be time for you to communicate with me, and I shall be glad to have your views. In the mean time you will of course proceed as though no modification of existing organization was contemplated.*

Hood had won. He would remain in command of the Army of Tennessee, with a nominal superior overseeing a larger department. He had also rid himself of a subordinate whom he no longer trusted and received final permission to embark on his proposed offensive. But his success carried with it a new responsibility. He would have to deliver a victory.[12]

Chapter 3

As Shots from a Magazine-Gun

M ajor General William Tecumseh Sherman was the hero of the day. While the North had enjoyed some small successes, such as the capture of Mobile Bay in early August, the war had reached a stalemate in the two main theaters, Virginia and Georgia. Sherman's victory at Atlanta changed that. In an instant, Lincoln's prospects for reelection improved dramatically. Northern newspapers heralded the victory. Grant ordered his artillery in front of Petersburg and Richmond to bombard the enemy trenches in salute, "firing a national salute, or thirty-six rounds from each battery. The firing commenced about eleven o clock. You cannot imagine either the sight or the sound. The pyrotechnical display would have done honor to the fourth of July, and the noise satisfied the most uproarious of urchins."[13]

The fall of Atlanta saw Sherman's armies deployed south of the city opposite Hood near Lovejoy Station. Sherman controlled three armies, in modern terms an army group, formally designated the Military Division of the Mississippi. However, this high-sounding title was rarely used among the troops. Each man considered himself a member of one of the three individual armies. The Army of the Cumberland, commanded by Major General George H. Thomas, was the largest of the three. It was further divided into three army corps: the Fourth, Fourteenth and Twentieth. The Fourth and Fourteenth were with Sherman outside Lovejoy, while the Twentieth had stayed behind and now occupied the city of Atlanta itself. Major General Oliver O. Howard's Army of the Tennessee—not to be confused with the Confederate Army *of* Tennessee—was the next largest. It also had three corps, but each corps was typically smaller than its Cumberland counterpart. These three corps were the Fifteenth, Sixteenth and Seventeenth Army Corps. Finally, the smallest was the Army of the Ohio, which was actually only one infantry corps, the Twenty-third, and one cavalry division. The corps was led by Major General John M. Schofield. In total, Sherman had about 81,758 men present for duty in and around Atlanta.[14]

Ultimately, Sherman decided against crushing Hood's army at Lovejoy, even though he outnumbered it at least two to one. He had achieved his goal—that is, capture the important railroad and industry hub of Atlanta and prevent Johnston or Hood from sending reinforcements to Lee in Virginia. The Confederates had a fairly strong position, although not one that couldn't be outflanked. However, with his objectives complete, Sherman saw no need for further bloodshed. Accordingly, on September 5, the Union armies began withdrawing. The Army of the Cumberland moved to occupy Atlanta. The Army of the Ohio marched to Decatur, a small city about eight miles east of the city, and the Army of the Tennessee took up a position at East Point southwest of Atlanta.[15]

Unfortunately, much as the conquest of Vicksburg had paralyzed the victorious Union army for months, Sherman's conquest of Atlanta brought about a period of stagnation and waiting. His armies were hardly prepared to resume prolonged offensive operations. First, the abovementioned evacuation and truce took up much of September. At the same time, Confederate cavalry commander Nathan Bedford Forrest appeared in northern Alabama with more than four thousand horsemen and captured the Union garrison at Athens. From there, he could threaten middle and western Tennessee. This required Sherman's attention as he shifted forces in his theater to counter the threat.

Next, many of his top commanders left the army. Major General John A. Logan, a staunch Democrat, headed north to stump for Lincoln's reelection. So did Major General Francis P. Blair Jr., brother of Lincoln's postmaster general. The two commanded the Fifteenth and Seventeenth Corps, respectively. In an unusual twist, one of the Sixteenth Corps' division commanders, Brigadier General Thomas W. Sweeney, was court-martialed and relieved of duty for getting into a fistfight with his commanding officer! The casualties of the campaign and the mustering out of units whose enlistments had expired drastically reduced the strength of many divisions and corps. This, combined with the loss of two experienced corps commanders, led Howard, with Sherman's approval, to reorganize the Army of the Tennessee. Temporary commanders were put in place of the Fifteenth and Seventeenth Corps, and the Sixteenth Corps was broken up. Sweeney's Second Division, now commanded by Brigadier General John M. Corse, went to the Fifteenth Corps, while the other division went to the Seventeenth.[16]

Still, Sherman's next move was never far from his mind. As early as September 10, he was making inquiries of Grant about the possibility of marching through the Confederate interior. To accomplish this, he asked if the U.S. Navy could clear either the Savannah River up to Augusta or the Chattahoochee to Columbus. Either would open a water route from which Sherman could draw supplies. Major General Henry W. Halleck, the army's chief of staff, suggested marching from Columbus through Montgomery and Selma, Alabama, and linking up with forces blocking the port of Mobile.

On the twentieth, Lieutenant Colonel Horace Porter, a trusted member of Grant's staff, arrived in Atlanta. Sherman met him cordially on the porch of his headquarters, coat unbuttoned, black hat slouched low on his head and feet comfortably ensconced in a pair of slippers. After introductions, the two spoke at length about the progress of the war, both east and west. Sherman would occasionally rise from his chair or stretch his legs, and he continually moved his feet in and out of the slippers. Porter was impressed with his vigor, noting that he exhibited "a strong individuality in every movement, and there was a peculiar energy of manner in uttering the crisp words and epigrammatic phrases which fell from his lips as rapidly as shots from a magazine-gun." Later, after much discussion between the two and Sherman's senior generals, Sherman spelled out his plan to march toward Savannah in a detailed letter to Grant. Letter in hand, along with Sherman's official report on the Atlanta Campaign, Porter left Atlanta on the twenty-seventh for the return trip to Virginia.[17]

Sherman viewed Hood's move from Jonesborough to Palmetto on the eighteenth with interest but not alarm. He was as aware of Hood's options as Hood. Still, he couldn't take the chance of the Confederates breaking the railroad ties to Chattanooga, and he took precautionary measures. On the twenty-fourth, he ordered Corse's Seventeenth Corps division to move from East Point to Rome—one brigade of the division was already there on garrison duty. The next day, he likewise sent a division from the Fourth Corps to bolster the garrison at Chattanooga. Information on his opponent's plans was readily forthcoming. Davis's trip to Hood's headquarters was common knowledge. In fact, he had already read newspapers detailing a speech Davis delivered in Macon. A spy brought him the contents of the

George N. Barnard photograph of Allatoona Pass looking north. The Star Fort is on top of the hill to the left. *National Archives, 533402.*

speech he delivered to the troops at Palmetto, as well as his designs on middle Tennessee. Even with this intelligence, Sherman could do nothing else, at least for the moment. He still needed time to build up supplies in Atlanta, and he had not yet worked out the details of, or received approval for, his future plans from Grant. If anyone was to take the initiative, it would have to be Hood. The gray cavalier would not disappoint.[18]

Chapter 4

Bring Relief to
Our Only Precious Cause

T he night of September 28 was cool in Palmetto but not cold enough
to form frost the next morning. That evening, General Hood issued
marching orders for the upcoming campaign. This included a directive for
the men to cook three days' rations, an activity that took most of the night.
Couriers dashed here and there, officers received their orders and the men
went through the now familiar routine for an advance. When morning came
on the twenty-ninth, the Army of Tennessee was ready to move.[19]

Major General Samuel G. French prepared his division for the march.
Born in Gloucester County, New Jersey, he graduated from West Point in
1843 alongside such notable future high-ranking Union officers as William
B. Franklin, Rufus Ingalls and, above all, Ulysses Grant. Serving in the
Mexican-American War, he was wounded at the Battle of Buena Vista.
Afterward, he married into and inherited ownership of a plantation in
Natchez, Mississippi, but sadly, his wife died in 1857 during the birth of
their second child. When Mississippi seceded in 1861, the governor of
Mississippi appointed French to the rank of lieutenant colonel and the
position of chief of ordnance in the army of the state of Mississippi.
Holding various commands in Virginia during the first years of the war,
he was transferred to Mississippi in June 1863 to command a division
in the forces gathering to relieve the siege of Vicksburg. While on sick
leave, his division was broken up, and he was assigned the nucleus of his
current division in October. He commanded this division throughout the
subsequent Atlanta Campaign.[20]

When Sherman left Chattanooga and began his advance in May 1864, French's Division was in Alabama scouring the countryside for deserters and enforcing conscript laws. The division was a new one, relatively speaking, compared to many of the other commands in the Army of Tennessee. While many of those divisions had been formed in the summer and fall of 1862, allowing them to march, sweat, bleed and bond together for almost two years, the nucleus of French's Division didn't come together until the fall of 1863; the division didn't take its current form until April the following year. It consisted of three brigades. The two original brigades were Cockrell's Brigade and Ector's Brigade, with Sears' Brigade joining them in Alabama.[21]

Few would argue that the Missourians of Cockrell's Brigade were one of the elite units in the Army of Tennessee, or any Confederate army for that matter. Forged in the bitter "civil war within a civil war" that was 1861 Missouri, the men had fought hard at Wilson's Creek and Pea Ridge, as well as some at Shiloh. Outside Corinth, they stormed the Union redoubts and briefly entered the town. At Vicksburg, they stood fast and even successfully charged against a vastly superior force at Port Gibson. Then they routed Union troops at Champion's Hill in a devastating counterattack that only failed for lack of support. At Big Black River, they held while others ran, only narrowly escaping. Their subsequent capture and exchange after the Siege of Vicksburg did little to dampen their ardor. In June, along the slopes of Kennesaw Mountain, they fought some of Sherman's toughest veterans to a standstill on Pigeon Hill. Now these Missourians, orphaned and with no way to return home while the war was being fought, were prepared once more to bring the fight to the enemy. The brigade had the remnants of eight regiments that had been consolidated down to four to ease in handling. They were the 1st and 4th, the 2nd and 6th and the 3rd and 5th Missouri Infantry and the 1st and 3rd Missouri Cavalry (dismounted). They were led by the equally competent and determined Brigadier General Francis Marion Cockrell.[22]

General Cockrell, a native of Warrensburg, Missouri, graduated from Chapel Hill College in 1853. Admitted to the state bar in 1855, he was a practicing lawyer in his hometown before the war began. Like French, he was a widower, his wife having died in 1859, leaving him with two sons. Opposed to secession, he nevertheless joined the Missouri Home Guard after the "Camp Jackson Massacre." He was immediately elected captain of his company and went on to fight at Wilson's Creek, Lexington and Pea Ridge. In May 1862, he was promoted to colonel of the 2nd Missouri and then rose to command the brigade in April 1863. It was under Cockrell that the brigade cemented its reputation during the Vicksburg Campaign.

He was a tall, imposing officer who inspired confidence in his men. As one newspaper reporter described him:

> *Cockrell's full height is six feet and an inch, his weight fully 215 pounds. He has a full, strong habit of body, capable of much labor and strain, mental and physical. He has a bold, aquiline face, long brown hair falling back from a high arched forehead, and a long brown moustache and goatee giving amplitude and shading to his features. His eyes are blue and animated and his complexion is clear, indicating temperance and health. His manner is hearty and free, with a touch of shrewdness. He has a bright smile in talking. He is a fine man to look at and a good one for a friend to trust to in seasons of doubt and danger.*

General French could count on Cockrell and his Missourians to carry out any task he called on them to perform.[23]

The men of Ector's Texas Brigade would dispute anyone trying to rank them second fiddle to the Missourians in the division. If they hadn't seen as many outright battles as Cockrell's men, the ones they had fought were marked with equally hard combat. The brigade consisted of six regiments: the 10th, 14th and 32nd Texas Cavalry (dismounted); the 9th Texas; and the 29th and 39th North Carolina. Most of these regiments had fought early in the war in Missouri or Shiloh or during the invasion of Kentucky in the fall of 1862. Under Brigadier General Matthew D. Ector, it had smashed the Union right at Stone's River. At Chickamauga, the brigade fought hard on the morning of the first day, suffering more than 50 percent casualties, relegating it to a supporting role on the second. It performed competently during the recent struggle for Atlanta, where General Ector was wounded in July. Command of the brigade passed to Colonel William H. Young of the 9th Texas, but it kept the sobriquet "Ector's Brigade" even after Young's promotion to brigadier general. It endured the day-to-day skirmishing and attrition during the siege of the city itself and pulled back with the army when it abandoned Atlanta.[24]

William Young was born in Boonesville, Missouri, but the family moved to Texas while he was still an infant, eventually settling in Grayson County. He attended colleges in Tennessee and Texas before ending up at the University of Virginia as the war commenced in 1861. Returning to Texas, he recruited an infantry company and was elected its captain. The company became part of the 9th Texas Infantry, and Young was promoted to colonel and command of the regiment after Shiloh. He fought with great distinction in all the regiment's subsequent battles. He was then wounded five times: once each at Stone's River, Jackson and Chickamauga and twice at Kennesaw Mountain. He returned to duty each time. He took command of the brigade after Ector's wounding and was promoted to brigadier general on August 15. The upcoming advance would be his first real test of leadership at the brigade level.[25]

The final infantry unit in the division was Sears' Brigade of Mississippians. It included six units: the 4th, 35th, 36th, 39th and 46th Mississippi Regiments, as well as the 7th Mississippi Battalion. The individual regiments of the brigade had a rough history. Some had fought at Corinth, some at Iuka and some at Chickasaw Bayou. All had been captured and exchanged at Vicksburg. One regiment, the 4th, had been captured and exchanged twice, once at Fort Donelson early in the war and again at Vicksburg. The brigade came together in approximately its current roster in October 1863 after the soldiers' exchanges. They were moved from various posts throughout Mississippi and Alabama during the winter and were formally assigned to French's Division in April 1864, completing its current incarnation.

Unfortunately, the Mississippians never fully recovered from their capture the previous year. During the Atlanta Campaign, the brigade had the highest rate of desertions and "captures" on the division skirmish line, at times thrice as many as their fellow Missourians and Texans. Some had no love lost for Hood either, even after two months. William Pitt Chambers of the 46th Mississippi wrote, "The removal of Gen. Johnston in July caused great indignation in our part of the army, at least, and the reverses that have since befallen us had tended neither to ally nor mollify the feeling. On the contrary, it seemed to be intensified, and hence it was with distrustful glances we looked upon our brave but rash commander-in-chief." The soldiers themselves, naturally, didn't feel as if they were doing anything less than their duty, but the statistics tell another story. There were units in the army with greater morale problems, but the best that could reasonably be expected from the Mississippians was probably holding the line. Their ability on the offensive was questionable.[26]

Commanding the Mississippians was Brigadier General Claudius W. Sears. Born in Peru, Massachusetts, he was a West Point graduate (class of 1841). He resigned his commission the following year and became an instructor at St. Thomas Hall in Holly Springs, Mississippi. He followed that up as a professor of mathematics at the University of Louisiana, now Tulane University, from 1845 to 1859, and then returned to St. Thomas as president until 1861. When war broke out, he enlisted in the

17th Mississippi and was elected captain of Company G. He fought with the regiment in Virginia during the battles of 1861 and 1862, including First Bull Run, Ball's Bluff, the Peninsula Campaign and Antietam. He was commissioned colonel of the 46th Mississippi in late 1862 and led the regiment at Chickasaw Bayou in December. Captured at Vicksburg, he wasn't exchanged for many months and didn't return to his command until 1864. When the previous brigade commander died after an accidental fall from his horse, Sears was promoted to brigadier general and brigade command on March 1. William Chambers thought highly of him at least, calling him a "trusted and beloved officer." Still, his inability to keep the brigade from melting away during the recent campaign left questions about his abilities or, at a minimum, confirmed his mediocrity.[27]

At the last recorded muster, on September 20, French's Division had 3,386 infantry present for duty. That included officers, teamsters, musicians, surgeons and anybody who marched with the division. However, the effective total, counting only those soldiers actually lugging a rifle and shooting at the enemy, was 2,962. That number probably hadn't changed too much in the intervening eight days, but it would diminish somewhat once the division started moving. Straggling and desertions tended to chip away at the strength of any army on the march, especially a recently defeated one. The division also had fire support in the form of an artillery battalion. The composition of this battalion was in flux, however, as individual batteries were being rotated out, most going to reserve at Macon.[28]

French's Division was one of three in Stewart's Corps. The other divisions were led by Major General William W. Loring and Major General Edward C. Walthall. Loring's Division, the largest in the corps, had about 4,551 men present for duty, while Walthall could count about 2,731. All told, the corps had approximately 11,567 present. There were two other infantry corps in the army under Lieutenant General Lee and Major General Benjamin F. Cheatham, who replaced Hardee after his relief. Most of Hood's cavalry was already in north Georgia and Alabama, and he only had one division of horsemen on hand at Palmetto, commanded by Brigadier General William H. Jackson. In total, the Army of Tennessee marched north with about 39,043 men present for duty, of which 33,780 were in the ranks on the firing line.[29]

The advance began early the next morning, Thursday, September 29. Jackson's cavalry division let the way. Cheatham's Corps moved out at 8:00 a.m., but French's Division and the rest of Stewart's Corps didn't begin marching until about 2:00 p.m. It was 9:00 p.m. before they reached the pontoon bridge spanning the Chattahoochee River. The night was dark, and there were men with torches lighting the way across the water. Some were stationed at each end of the bridge and others at intervals on the span itself. There was a great sag in the middle, but the bridge held up fine, and there was no trouble crossing. Once over, the corps kept marching another five miles before camping for the night. Jackson's Division and army headquarters, in advance of the rest of the men, stopped at Pray's Church. The day ended with Jackson, Lee and Stewart's men across the river. Cheatham's Corps remained on the south side.[30]

The march resumed in the morning. Jackson's cavalry left at 7:00 a.m. and headed toward Powder Springs. Hood and his headquarters remained at Pray's Church until about 1:00 p.m. and then moved to a small hamlet with the ominous name of Dark Corner. Stewart's Corps marched about fifteen miles and made camp at Brownsville at 2:00 p.m. On October 1, Stewart and Lee remained in camp while Cheatham caught up. It rained incessantly throughout the day.[31]

That morning, Hood invited all the present corps and division commanders to his headquarters. When General French arrived, Stewart, Loring and Walthall were already present. So were Lee and two of his division commanders. According to French, as soon as he entered the headquarters, Hood engaged him.

"General French, what do you think General Sherman will do now?" he asked.

"I suppose," French replied, "he will turn southwest and move on to Mobile: or he may go to Augusta to destroy our powder mills, and then make for Charleston or Savannah."

"In that event do you believe he can sustain his troops on the march if our cavalry lay waste the country before him?"

"He will find all he wants as he moves on."

"Well, I have nothing to do with that," said Hood, "as the President has promised to attend to that matter."

Unfortunately, French was in the minority opinion. Only Lee agreed somewhat with him, but he thought the Federal cavalry would be able to supply itself on the march well enough. French then went on to advocate throwing the entire Army of Tennessee on the railroad north of Kennesaw and chafed at the delay. Hood had other plans. He issued orders for the forthcoming days, which were to be passed down the chain of command to their brigade and regimental commanders. The meeting broke up, and the officers returned to their commands.[32]

French wasn't alone with his disaffection for Hood's plans. Robert Patrick, a commissary in Stewart's Corps, lamented the want of attention given to feeding the army:

> *We have orders to move very early in the morning but there are no bread rations for the troops here yet. They were to have been here early in the afternoon but they have not yet arrived and I do not know how the men can march without something to eat. They have meat rations for tomorrow of bacon. General Hood or somebody else at the head of affairs doesn't seem to understand his business.* [33]

Yet one of the stalwart Missourians in Cockrell's Brigade noted in his diary entry for the day that they "were in very good spirits and all hopeful that our expedition will turn out successfully and bring relief to our only precious Cause." Logistic hiccups aside, Hood was doing all he could to justify that faith. [34]

Chapter 5

We Shall Be "Minute Men"

Stealing a march on an enemy requires luck, skill and an army with a good deal of discipline. Unfortunately for Hood, he had one out of three at best, and if the results of the last campaign counted for anything, he may have lacked all three. In this case, it was the Army of Tennessee's morale problem and lack of discipline that revealed his hand to Sherman when they left their fortifications at Palmetto and began the trek north of the Chattahoochee.

As the Confederate army marched toward the bridges spanning the river, those tired of the bloodshed, fatigue and hunger either stayed behind or made their way toward the Yankee lines. General Howard's infantry at East Point, being the closest to the Rebels, eagerly picked them up and were the first to report on Hood's suspected movement. Interestingly, a division of Federal cavalry lay between Hood and Howard, yet its commander reported nothing of the enemy's movements or deserters. Howard, on the other hand, immediately sent a telegram to Sherman, informing him that Hood had begun marching north toward the Chattahoochee as early as 5:00 a.m.[35]

The news triggered a burst of activity at Sherman's headquarters. First, the commanding general had to make decisions based on what Hood might do. He knew Hood had two options: he could either move north against the railroad and Sherman's supply line, or he could move west toward Alabama and be in a position to threaten the Union garrisons there and in Tennessee. The last was a real threat, because Forrest and Confederate cavalry commander Joseph Wheeler were already endangering the railroad in that area. Sherman had already moved two infantry divisions north from Atlanta to bolster the garrisons behind him. The possibility of Hood's entire army moving in that direction spurred Sherman to an even greater decision. He ordered General Thomas to relinquish field command of the Army of the Cumberland to Major General David S. Stanley, travel to Chattanooga and take command of all the forces in Tennessee and northern Alabama. Sherman had, the previous evening, ordered yet another infantry division from Atlanta to accompany him, this time from the Fourteenth Corps. Thomas left at noon, and the infantry were loaded on cars and headed north that same day.[36]

That still left the railroad south of Chattanooga as Sherman's responsibility. Posted along that iron lifeline was a string of fortifications and garrisons assigned to protect it. Most were drawn from Howard's Army of the Tennessee, and the major towns had at least some infantry stationed in them. North of the Chattahoochee, a small garrison protected the area around Marietta and Kennesaw Mountain. Corse's Fourth Division was at Rome, and Smith's Third was in Cartersville guarding the railroad bridge over the Etowah River, as well as the pass at Allatoona. Farther north, there was a major garrison at Resaca guarding the railroad bridge over the Oostanaula. There was at least some form of protection at each major railroad bridge and even at the smaller bridges that crossed insignificant creeks and brooks. After all, if Confederate cavalry or guerillas burned even a small bridge, it would break the rail line and cause major delays until the structure could be rebuilt. Most of these bridges were guarded by stout wooden blockhouses, in which small garrisons could easily cover the bridges with rifle fire and discourage bushwhackers and partisans. Larger, more elaborate earthen forts guarded the bridges over the Etowah and Oostanaula.

In addition to sending Thomas north, Sherman and his subordinates began notifying the garrisons of Hood's movements. Howard requested of Brigadier William Vandever, the commander at Marietta, that he establish a system of "vigilant pickets and patrols" up to three miles out. Sherman tasked Brigadier General John McArthur, whom Vandever had relieved only two days before but who was still in the Marietta area, to supervise the defense of the small outpost on top of Kennesaw Mountain. Sherman also reminded John E. Smith at Cartersville that he "cannot be too particular about Allatoona, and about Pumpkin Vine [Creek]," as Hood could still move either there or toward Alabama.[37]

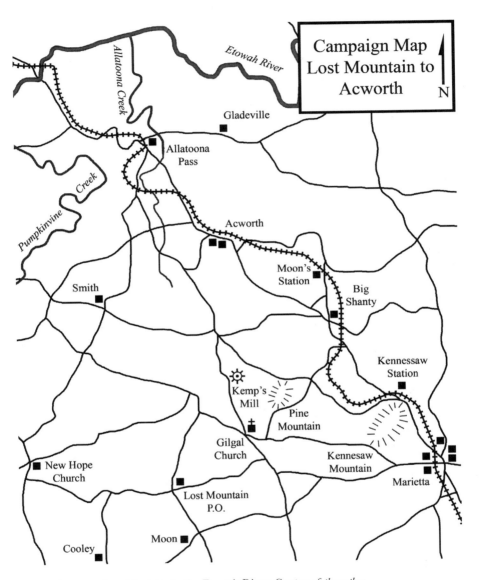

Campaign map from Marietta to the Etowah River. *Courtesy of the author.*

One important, and often overlooked, asset available to Sherman was his Signal Corps. These specialists were tasked with keeping communications open between the various posts and commands of the army. Not only did this include the static garrisons in towns and fortifications, but it also meant moving with the army and setting up tactical communications between commanders in the field—more often at the army and corps level but sometimes down to division commanders as well. There were four primary means of communication available to commanders at the time. Verbal and written orders were the responsibility of and primary mode of communications between the smaller regimental, brigade and division commands. The Signal Corps was composed of trained specialists who communicated by electronic telegraph or, alternatively, a system of flags. The telegraph operators worked out of small permanent outposts in major towns, but they also used mobile wagons that could move with the army and set up a communication network in the field. This linked an army commander and his subordinates to one another in real time, faster than a courier could travel on horseback, and was an overlooked revolution in a war packed with technological breakthroughs.

If telegraph communications broke down, the operators could talk to one another over great distances using signal flags. A flagman would hold two flags, normally six feet square, at different positions using his arms, and each position represented a number. Each number, or series of numbers, would represent a letter. To prevent the enemy from reading the visual transmissions, the signals were coded, with both the sender and recipient maintaining codebooks to translate the messages. In this way, words could be transmitted as far as the eye could see, often from high ground using telescopes. The Confederates had a similar flag system, and each side regularly broke and read the other's cyphers. The South also had a telegraph network, but its tactical implementation on the army level was nowhere near as sophisticated as the more technologically advanced North.[38]

There was a telegraph and signal station on top of Kennesaw Mountain, the site McArthur was assigned to protect. From Kennesaw, the station could view and report on the activities of any force for miles in any direction. It could relay information down to the town of Marietta at the eastern base of the mountain or north toward Allatoona. Fortuitously, General Howard on the twenty-eighth ordered his Signal Corps detachment to report to the Army of the Cumberland and bolster Sherman's communications assets. Lieutenant Charles H. Fish commanded the detail, and the men loaded their equipment into their wagon early the next morning. Soon the "little army of seven," as Fish called it, began its trek north from East Point to Atlanta. Upon reaching Atlanta in the afternoon, Fish reported to Captain Samuel Bachtell. Bachtell then ordered him to continue on to Kennesaw the next day to reinforce the station there. A few miles south of the railroad bridge over the Etowah River, the Western & Atlantic ran through the Allatoona Mountains, a small range of hills nestled in that region of northern Georgia. The most prominent feature along the line was the large railroad cut at Allatoona Pass. From the heights at the pass, men could see and communicate by signal flag with the station on top of Kennesaw. The fourteen-man Signal Corps squad stationed there was commanded by Lieutenant John Q. Adams.[39]

The weak link in Sherman's assets, at least in his own opinion, was his cavalry. He had three cavalry divisions at his disposal, under the nominal command of Brigadier General Washington L. Elliott. Brigadier General Edward M. McCook led the First Division, which was spread out between Cartersville, Calhoun and farther north into Tennessee as it refitted and regrouped. Brigadier General Kenner Garrard commanded the Second Division, stationed at Blake's Mill (near the modern-day intersection of Interstate 85 and Shallowford Road) and which had only recently returned from a reconnaissance north of the Chattahoochee near Acworth, Canton and Roswell. The Third Division was helmed by Brigadier General Judson Kilpatrick. A controversial figure (he was nicknamed "Kil-Cavalry"), Kilpatrick had previously ordered a suicidal and unnecessary cavalry charge at Gettysburg, and early in 1864, he led a disastrous raid near Richmond. The Third Division was currently at Patterson's Cross Roads southwest of East Point (close to modern-day Deerwood Park), watching the Confederate army.[40]

The cavalry divisions were not grouped into a traditional corps. Elliott's actual title was "Chief of Cavalry," a sure indication of Sherman's opinion of his subordinate's abilities. In fact, Elliott rarely accompanied his divisions in the field and never led from the front. During the Atlanta Campaign, Sherman had a habit of bypassing Elliott and issuing orders to the cavalry division commanders directly. The three divisions, as well as their commanders, fared little better in Sherman's estimation. He made no secret of the disdain in which he held his cavalry leaders and actively sought to replace them. In fact, on September 23, Sherman had wired Grant a scathing telegram asking for any number of cavalry, even infantry, officers to replace those he currently had:

I do want very much a good cavalry officer to command, and have been maneuvering three months to get Mower here, but Canby has sent him up White River. My present cavalry need infantry guards and pickets, and it is hard to get them within ten miles of the front. If you think Ayres will do, I would like him. Romeyn B. Ayres is, or was, as bad a growler as Granger. I would prefer Gregg or Wilson; still, anybody with proper rank will be better than Garrard. Kilpatrick is well enough for small scouts, but I do want a man of sense and courage to manage my cavalry, and will take any one that you have tried.

Not exactly a glowing review of his subordinates. Still, for the time being, Sherman would have to work with what he had.[41]

Sherman informed Elliott of Hood's movement as soon as he learned of it from Howard, and then he pushed him to get his cavalry moving. He told Elliott that he wanted Garrard to link up with Kilpatrick and that both should scout out and get information on the enemy. "Our cavalry must do more," prodded Sherman, "for it is strange Forrest and Wheeler should circle around us thus. We should at least make ten miles to his hundred." Garrard only had one brigade to spare. After the reconnaissance, the rest of the division needed time to care for and re-shoe the horses. He immediately ordered his First Brigade under Major William H. Jennings to march to Kilpatrick and cooperate with him, and off they went.[42]

Kilpatrick started the morning of the thirtieth skirmishing sharply with Confederates south of the Chattahoochee, attempting to push toward the Rebels still on the south side. He lost two men killed and five wounded, as well as a number of horses. When he informed Sherman of the scuffle, the commander in chief directed Elliott to have Kilpatrick disregard the Rebels on the south side and immediately cross his entire command to the north of the river and search for the Confederates there. He was more interested in finding out where Hood was going, not what was left at his old camp.[43]

Sherman spent the last day of September keeping up with his infantry commands and dictating further orders. Thomas informed Sherman that the rail line was jammed with men traveling to and returning from furlough, as well as the movement of infantry to threatened points along the supply line. Sherman ordered all of his infantry commands to end furloughs immediately. He also coordinated a plan of action with Thomas in case Hood moved into Alabama. He also sent instructions to Brigadier General Jacob D. Cox in Decatur, commanding the Army of the Ohio while Schofield was up north directing affairs in the rest of his department. Sherman wanted Cox to be ready to move at a moment's notice. Cox replied enthusiastically that "we shall be 'minute men' in the contingency." Sherman also heard from Corse and McArthur. Corse reported that civilians had told him that Hood was across the Chattahoochee and at Villa Rica—true, as Dark Corner is a few miles east of the town. McArthur also corroborated this bit of intelligence. Deserters and civilians told him that Hood had crossed the river in three columns. Civilians recounted that Rebel soldiers informed them that they were headed toward Rome. All this information helped Sherman form a clearer picture of Hood's movements.[44]

The next day, October 1, Sherman sent Grant a telegram updating him on the turn of events in Georgia. In it, he succinctly put forth the idea that if Hood was headed toward Alabama and parts north, he would prefer to let Thomas and the forces at his disposal deal with it while he laid waste to Atlanta and marched to Savannah:

> *Hood is evidently on the WEST side of Chattahoochee below Sweet Water. If he tries to get on my road* [railroad] *this side of the Etowah I shall attack him, but if he goes over to the Selma and Talladega road why would it not do for me to leave Tennessee to the force which Thomas has and the reserves soon to come to Nashville, and for me to destroy Atlanta, and them march across Georgia to Savannah or Charleston, breaking roads and doing irreparable damage? We cannot remain on the defensive.*

Sherman was thinking aggressively, and he wanted his subordinates to do the same. When Elliott told him that Kilpatrick was holding the line of Sweet Water Creek, a tributary north of the Chattahoochee that forms a natural barrier between the two forces, Sherman replied that he was not interested in picket lines or holding territory. He wanted the cavalry to move forward and envelope the enemy, finding out exactly where they are headed. While Elliott quibbled about a small one-hundred-man detachment left at Patterson's Cross Roads, Sherman brushed the concern aside and ordered Howard to send two entire infantry divisions south on a reconnaissance.[45]

Kilpatrick, for his part, had another busy day. The bridges across Sweet Water and Noyes Creek, a northern extension of Sweet Water that stretched all the way to Kennesaw Mountain, were all burned, and the streams were too swollen to ford. Nevertheless, Kilpatrick's men swam Sweet Water at one o'clock but were driven back to the east side after a firefight. Undeterred, the cavalrymen tried again three hours later, this time with artillery support. They succeeded in establishing themselves on the west bank and began constructing a bridge. Kilpatrick continued to hope that Garrard's First Brigade would arrive and cover his northern right flank, but it did not arrive. Despite his previous misguided foray south of the river, north of it he was doing his best to cross the natural and man-made barriers to his front. Bypassing Elliott, as was his style, Sherman reiterated to Kilpatrick his desire for the cavalry to "develop Hood's design."[46]

Sherman was loath to let Hood maintain the initiative, but to a point; he had to first find out where the Confederate was going before he could order the appropriate response. Regardless, he wasn't about to let his men remain idle. He ordered Howard to march two divisions of his army to Fairburn, a small town on the railroad midway between East Point and Palmetto. He also told Cox to send a division from Decatur to Flat Rock. He explained to both army commanders what he told Grant: if Hood goes to Alabama, they will march to Savannah. The idea of a march through the heartland was firmly entrenched in Sherman's mind. He only had to wait for the right moment to implement it.[47]

The garrisons along the railroad continued to communicate with their commander in chief. Sherman wired Smith at Cartersville of Hood's potential movements and instructed him to hold the Etowah bridge and Allatoona securely. He did the same to Corse and told him that, if necessary, he was to leave a small garrison at Rome and move with the bulk of his division to reinforce Smith. Corse replied to Sherman that there had not been any enemy activity within twenty-five miles of Rome. Sherman again told McArthur to keep his men well at hand. If Hood tried to break the railroad between Marietta and the Etowah, Sherman would march with his whole army from Atlanta to meet him.[48]

Lieutenant Fish and his seven-man army arrived in Marietta the evening of September 30 and slept at the headquarters of General Vandever. The next morning, after Fish secured rations and supplies for his men, they headed to the summit of Kennesaw. Once there, he reported to Lieutenant James H. Connolly, the ranking officer manning the signal station. As Fish stood at the crest, a torrent of emotions washed over him. Here he stood atop the earthworks that only three months before had contained "frowning batteries…that looked down upon us with such perfect contempt." His thoughts turned to the brave men who had assaulted the heights that sanguine day, June 27, only to be forever laid to rest before the sun set. Then he began to question his assignment. Why did it take two signal officers to man a now unimportant station behind the lines? He would soon find out.[49]

For the moment, though, all was quiet. At 11:00 a.m., he signaled Bachtell, currently establishing a station at Vining's Hill near the railroad bridge across the Chattahoochee, that all was well. He did it again at 9:00 p.m. Lieutenant Adams, from his post at Allatoona, reported to Bachtell at six o'clock that all was quiet. That would change dramatically over the next few days.[50]

Chapter 6

The Yanks Had His Hogs

N estled comfortably in the low Allatoona Mountains, the southernmost extension of the Appalachians, lies the small town of Allatoona. A small settlement, it consisted of six or seven houses in 1864. It was also one of the more important garrisons on the Western & Atlantic Railroad. A locally important transportation hub, two relatively low ridges from the east and south met at the site and allowed for an easy crossing of the Allatoona range. Not surprisingly, two important roads intersected at the town. One, the Sandtown or Tennessee Road, came up from the south. It was an old Cherokee Indian trail that originated at Sandtown and Montgomery Ferry on the Chattahoochee River, crossed the Allatoona Mountains at the pass and continued north to Tennessee. The other, the Old Alabama Road, went east–west. A few miles west of Allatoona, the road split. The Old Alabama Road continued west along the south bank of the Etowah, and the Cartersville Road went north and crossed the Etowah near the railroad bridge. In fact, the road was often referred to as the "Cartersville Road" by the residents of Allatoona village, and the soldiers stationed there took up the name.[51]

The coming of the Western & Atlantic Railroad increased the importance of the village. Just north of the town stood a prominent ridge. Instead of having the line follow the Cartersville Road, the owners of the railroad decided to blast a path straight through the ridge, bedrock and all. The result was a massive gorge cut through the hillside. The first 80 feet of the cut took away the earth and topsoil. The engineers then blasted a narrower

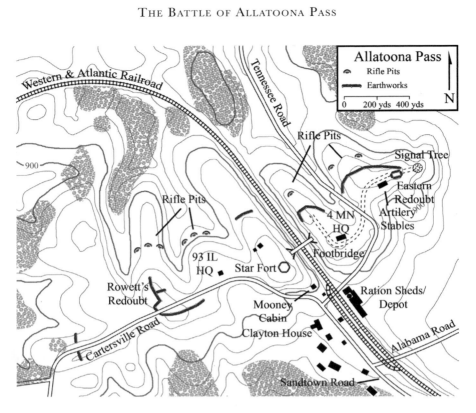

Map of Allatoona Pass and its fortifications. *Courtesy of the author.*

channel through 95 feet of bedrock, giving the cut a stepped appearance. The finished cut was 175 feet deep, 360 feet long and an average of 60 feet wide. It was an impressive engineering feat at the time, and only the tunnel at Tunnel Hill proved more difficult to build. A depot and water tower were soon built at the site.[52]

The war, as well as Sherman's campaign through the state, increased the importance of the village. The cut was a natural choke point along the railroad. Whoever held the cut controlled the flow of supplies along the line. Destroying it would impair traffic along the line more significantly than merely destroying miles of ties and metal rails, all of which could be replaced and repaired. General Johnston had attempted to hold the pass during the campaign. However, Sherman, who was stationed in the area in his early career, understood the importance of the terrain at the location. He therefore elected to bypass the fortifications that Johnston constructed there and march for Dallas to the southwest. Once the Confederates abandoned the cut, Sherman set about fortifying it even more. In June, he tasked his chief engineer, Colonel Orlando M. Poe, with the job.[53]

The terrain and fortifications around Allatoona could be divided into two sectors, east and west, conveniently bisected by the railroad. The eastern sector rose sharply from the cut to a hill. Atop this hill was a house that served as the headquarters for the 4th Minnesota, one of the regiments stationed there. A spur of the hill extended north, paralleling the railroad and the cut. To the east, the hill descended into a gentle saddle. The Tennessee Road left Allatoona, bisected the saddle below and continued north. Past the saddle, the ground again rose gently to the summit of another hill. The draw north of the saddle and between the two hills was sharp and long. The change in elevation between the two hilltops was minor, but the slopes of the hill itself were quite steep. The grade to the north was uphill, to be sure, but manageable. However, the slopes to the east and south were steep and, at points, quite precipitous. The land fell quickly in these areas into the valley of Allatoona Creek.[54]

The fortifications in this sector of the garrison were focused on the easternmost hilltop. There, Poe constructed a strong earthen fort, about sixty-five feet long and fifty feet wide. It had walls twelve feet thick and was surrounded by a ditch six feet deep. As a practical matter, this made the wall of the fort twelve feet tall, and it could only be climbed with scaling ladders. It was accurately, if unimaginatively, dubbed the Eastern Redoubt. Along the northern slope, starting near the redoubt, the men built a line of earthworks stretching all the way to the Tennessee Road. Another U-shaped half-fort was built along the northern slope of the spur next to the cut. There were no works at the saddle, but soldiers firing from the trenches near the Tennessee Road and the spur could support one another, covering the gap. Rifle pits that could fit one to three soldiers, what today would be called foxholes, were built farther out in all directions. Abatis were constructed and placed around and in front of each fortification and trench. These were made by felling trees and brush and laying them out so that the branches pointed toward the enemy. Any force that attacked the entrenchments would have to stop, or would at least be slowed down, due to the entanglements. This pause would often give the defenders time to fire a few more shots at the stalled enemy, a few more shots that could make all the difference in breaking and halting an assault.[55]

A few dozen yards east of the Eastern Redoubt, the men of the Signal Corps established a flag station atop a sixty-foot pine tree. Planks were nailed to the trunk of the tree to serve as rungs, and a wooden platform was built near the top. From the top of this station, the garrison could signal Kennesaw Mountain. The men also built a wooden building eighteen by forty feet, southeast of the fort, as a stable for the artillery horses. A footpath ran along the top of the ridge and connected the various stations from the headquarters building to the signal station.[56]

In the western sector, the cut rose to a hill directly west of the railroad and opposite the hill on which stood the 4th Minnesota's headquarters building. On this hill, Poe built another strong earthen fort. It had six sides and was roughly hexagonal in shape. It was about seventy-five feet long and sixty feet wide and was constructed with interlocking railroad ties. As with the Eastern Redoubt, the walls were twelve feet thick and twelve feet tall from the bottom of the six-foot ditch surrounding the structure. This fort was named the Star Fort. Artillery fire, and to a lesser extent small arms, from the two main redoubts interlocked and covered the depot and village to the south, as well as approaches from the north.[57]

A spur branched off from the hilltop and extended north. It paralleled the railroad; in fact, it paralleled the spur on the eastern side. A small trench covered the northern approach along this spur, and men stationed along these spurs could shoot over the railroad cut and cover one another with rifle fire. There was a small house about thirty yards north of the Star Fort.[58]

West of the Star Fort, the hill sloped down into a long ridge. The Cartersville Road ran north from the village, cut into the steep hillside and then turned west and followed this ridge. About four hundred yards west of the fort, the ridge rose slightly, and a house occupied the rise. A steep ravine ran to the north of this rise, between the northern spur and the house. The ridge and road continued west and rose to another gentle height two hundred yards farther. Past this elevation, the ridge immediately narrowed to a point only about ten yards wide, the width of the Cartersville Road, with steep ravines running to the north and south. To cover this narrow point, the men built another line of works on the slight rise. They extended north of the road, crossed it and then angled back almost due east to cover the southern approaches to the position. It was a naturally strong redoubt. There was a bastion, complete with opening for artillery, where the redoubt crossed the road, and a traverse built at right angles to the earthworks provided protection in case they were outflanked from the north. The slopes to the west and south were steep, and the only easy avenue of approach was along the road, which narrowed just in front of the redoubt. More abatis and entanglements were placed out front to further delay an approaching enemy.[59]

About four hundred yards farther west of this redoubt, the Cartersville Road turned sharply south. Two small redoubts covered the approaches to this area. They were probably part of Johnston's old line from the previous May. The men occupied the redoubts and dug a line of rifle pits in this area to give an early warning of any attack from that direction. In many places between this location and the Star Fort, the Cartersville Road dug into slopes and formed natural cuts and shelters for concealing infantry. In addition, the entire hillside, from the valley of Allatoona Creek to the east to the rifle pits at the curve on the Cartersville Road to the west, was clear-cut of all trees. This provided an open field of fire for all the entrenched positions in all directions. However, by October, the hillsides had become covered in low underbrush. Combined with natural folds in the terrain, not to mention the hundreds of tree stumps, this left plenty of cover and concealment to a foe willing to go to ground. Then again, a force that goes to ground isn't going to be charging and taking its objective.[60]

The railroad cut was an imposing physical barrier between the two sectors. The men constructed a bridge to facilitate traffic across the gorge and eliminate the need to walk down one slope and back up the other. About seventy-five feet north of the Star Fort, two pine trees were felled and laid across the cut, about ninety-five feet above the tracks. Planks were then nailed to the trunks and handrails added. The tents of the garrison dotted the hillsides. They took up most of the flat spaces along the rides, such as the area north and northwest of the Star Fort, along the crest of the ridge near the 4th Minnesota headquarters building and in front of the Eastern Redoubt.[61]

All of these strong fortifications would be useless dirt and logs without soldiers to man them. By early October, there were three regiments, a battery of artillery and a section of cavalry stationed at the pass. The infantry consisted of half of the First Brigade, Third Division, Fifteenth Army Corps. This included the 93rd Illinois, the 18th Wisconsin and the 4th Minnesota Infantry Regiments. The 12th Wisconsin Battery provided the artillery firepower, with four three-inch ordnance rifles and two twelve-pounder Napoleon smoothbores. Fifteen troopers from the 5th Ohio Cavalry gave the garrison a small resource of mounted scouts and couriers. The men were tough midwesterners and had fought variously at Shiloh, Iuka and Vicksburg. However, since the close of that campaign, the units had been held in reserve or relegated to garrison duty at various outposts. The exception was the Illinoisans, who had stormed Missionary Ridge at Chattanooga and lost heavily. In addition, the 4th Minnesota had been steadily receiving new

Barnard photograph of Allatoona Village from the Star Fort. Moore's Hill, the location of the Confederate artillery, is at the upper right. *National Archives, 528852.*

Modern location of the Allatoona blockhouse, indicated by the circle. *Photo by author.*

recruits and conscripts over the course of the summer, the last eighty just on October 1, so perhaps half of the regiment had never fired a shot in anger. In total, the outpost numbered about 1,092 officers and men.[62]

Two miles to the south, the railroad crossed Allatoona Creek. There, a sturdy wooden blockhouse stood guard over the bridge. Three companies (E, F and I) of the 18th Wisconsin watched over the crossing. There were about eighty-two men in the small command.[63]

While he was not the actual brigade commander, Lieutenant Colonel John E. Tourtellotte of the 4th Minnesota led the forces at Allatoona. The formal brigade commander, Colonel Joseph B. McCown, was with the balance of the unit north of the Etowah. Tourtellotte began the war as the captain of Company H and led it through Iuka, Corinth and Hatchie's Bridge. On October 12, 1862, the men elected him lieutenant colonel of the regiment, and he took over command on September 23, 1863, when their colonel was promoted to brigadier general. "He was a gallant and able commander," his men eulogized him long after the war, "a strict disciplinarian, always neat and tidy in his appearance and dress. His walk was erect and his bearing dignified and courtly." As he was the senior officer present, command of the garrison fell to Tourtellotte.[64]

Life at the garrison was slow. When they weren't being dispatched to other points on the railroad, the men merely stayed at the post. The exception was foraging. It was easy enough to survive on hardtack, army beef and desiccated vegetables, but naturally, a varied diet improved both health and morale. The formal process was for an armed party to venture into the countryside with a wagon, or wagons, and requisition food and supplies from the outlying farms. The owner was supposed to receive a receipt, which he could turn in to the federal government for payment at a later date. The truth, however, was that the necessities would be taken even if the farmer refused. Acceptance of the receipt really wasn't an option.

For the foragers, the expedition was risky. The locals didn't take too kindly to their food and belongings being confiscated, and neither did the Confederate government (although in truth, it did the same thing to its own citizens). Patrols of Confederate cavalry were always a threat. If a soldier wandered too far away from the party, he risked being captured or killed. A large enough Confederate patrol could capture an entire foraging party. All this meant a trip to a Confederate prison or worse if the captors were feeling less charitable. Therefore, foraging parties were quite large, and individual soldiers or small groups were forbidden from venturing into the countryside without permission.

Still, that did stop intrepid soldiers from skirting the rules. It never has and probably never will. John Laraba of the 4th Minnesota and his messmates, five in all, decided to venture out to see what they could find to improve their fare. They received a pass from Colonel Tourtellotte to pick blackberries just outside the picket lines. As soon as they passed outside the lines, they made for the Etowah River and its fertile valley. They eventually came upon a farm with a pen of four "nice, fat hogs." Not wanting to make any noise to alert the farmer, they decided to smash the hogs' heads in with fence rails. This, of course, didn't work, and soon the hogs were running about squealing and causing quite a racket. The party sent Laraba to intercept anyone who might come from the household to investigate, while they butchered the two best hogs. Sure enough, an old farmer and three or four black servants came to investigate. When the old man told Laraba that he had come to see what was wrong with his hogs, he replied that "the Yanks had his hogs, and that he had better about-face and forward march." The party took the hint and returned to the house.

The group put the hogs on poles and began the eight-mile return journey at nightfall. At some point, the men heard the tramp of horse and hid in the underbrush alongside the road. Soon a group of about eighty horsemen galloped past. After that close call, the men resumed their march. At about midnight, they ran into an outpost of their own men, far in advance of where they should be. The sentries fired on them and then turned and ran back to their lines. After a short discussion, Laraba's companions decided that it was no use to try to sneak through. They elected to own up to the consequences and "marched in boldly and faced the music."

Once they got in safely, the captain in charge of the picket line, from another regiment, related what had happened. The Confederate cavalry had blundered into the picket lines, starting a short firefight. The horsemen were driven off. This raised the alarm in the whole garrison. The picket lines were strengthened, and advanced parties were thrown out for extra security and early warning. These would-be foragers had caused a lot of trouble, the captain admonished, and he took their names, camp and regiment. A cold rain began falling, so he told the five of them to turn in and get ready for the next day.

As they got their bunks ready, one of the messmates suggested that they try a little strategy on the captain. They took a hindquarter of a hog and took it over to the captain's cook. They told him to prepare a good breakfast with it, along with a few sweet potatoes they brought along, as a present from the 4th Minnesota. That was the last they heard of their escapade.[65]

Laraba and his companions were lucky. Not so for Lorenzo Hopkins of the 93rd Illinois. On September 3, ten men, including Lorenzo, were captured by Rebel cavalry while foraging about six miles east of Allatoona. They also got the army wagon and its six-mule team. By the eighth, the Confederates had moved the prisoners about seventy miles southeast of Atlanta. That night, Lorenzo made his escape into the heavy timber and undergrowth near the camp. Avoiding patrols with bloodhounds and cavalry and hiding in canebrakes, he managed to elude capture. With the help of friendly black residents, who supplied him with cornbread, he made his way into the Union lines at Atlanta after three days. On September 11, he reunited with his regiment at Allatoona. He was one of those few lucky ones who managed to escape his captors.[66]

Unfortunately for Lorenzo, Laraba and their companions, their excitement was far from over. Allatoona lay square in the sights of Hood and his army.

Chapter 7

To Destroy Is a Soldier's Joy

O ne of the first things General Hood did the morning of the second was to send a telegram to General Bragg, now Davis's military adviser:

> *To-night my right will be at Powder Springs with my left at Lost Mountain. This will, I think, force the enemy to move on me or to move south. Should he move toward Augusta all available troops should be sent there, with an able officer of high rank to command. Could General Lee spare a division for that place in such an event?*

If Hood could not spare a division to protect a city in his own department, did he think Lee could do so while covering both the area around Richmond and the Shenandoah Valley? Either Hood was, to put it politely, throwing refuse against the wall to see if anything would stick, or he failed to grasp the strategic situation faced by himself and commanders on other fronts. One ploy exhibited desperation and the other ignorance. Neither portended success in an army commander.[67]

Another thing Hood did that morning was distribute a circular to his troops. The men were formed in line, and the regimental commanders addressed their men. According to one Rebel, their colonel "says Gen. Hood requested him to say to his men, that we are going to flank Sherman out of Atlanta, and in maneuvering we might be short of rations occasionally, but that he (Genl Hood) would do his best on that point. That he expected to have some fighting and some hard marching, and wanted an expression of the men upon it." Of course, out of hope or simply duty, every man said that he would go, at least publicly. Privately, others expressed their doubts. Robert Patrick feared that "this campaign will prove a failure though I will continue to hope for the best. I have no confidence in Hood's abilities. He is a good, rough fighter, but when that is said, all is said. He hasn't the knowledge of military affairs that Johnston possessed."[68]

Soon the camps broke up, and the army began to move. Army headquarters, along with Cheatham and Lee's Corps, marched north to Flint Hill Church. Stewart's men, on the other hand, remained to the east of the bulk of the army. They ended the day in the vicinity of the Moon House, a few miles south of the Lost Mountain Post Office. The area was familiar to them. They had spent May 24 there, as they marched to intercept Sherman south of the Etowah River. The cavalry brigade under Brigadier General Frank C. Armstrong was also very active. A small detachment made it to the railroad near Big Shanty. There they captured and burned a Union train. It was certainly enough to alarm McArthur, who notified Sherman immediately and requested additional reinforcements.[69]

William Chambers remembered one aspect of the day's march quite clearly: the sighting of an old landmark. "The direction of our route had so changed that we were travelling a little east of north, and when the air was clear we could [see] the bulk of Kennesaw mountain in the distance." The day was less cheerful for others. Robert Patrick still had to contend with a supply chain in disarray. Nothing seemed to work correctly. The wagon trains were intermixed, nobody seemed to know where to find anything or anybody, and as division commissary officer, there were no bread rations for him to issue to the men. The steady, organized hand of Johnston was missed.[70]

Life in the military is a dangerous business. Death can make its presence felt far from the whistling of bullets or the roar of cannons. Disease takes its toll, for sure, but nature adds it name to the butcher's bill as well. Just ask Captain Samuel T. Foster. As that Sunday drew to a close, the men stacked arms, all laid out nicely in a row. There was but one small thunderhead in the sky, not enough to yet notice, but shortly thereafter, "a Keen clap of thunder, the lightning striking the stack of guns, comes without any warning." The stack of guns was scattered to the wind. Some were bent and others broken. Many were simply knocked aside. Foster, standing about ten feet away from the strike, was carried through the air and landed upright about five feet away. Others were less fortunate. One boy in his company fell with foam bubbling from his mouth. The men immediately

The Cartersville Road cutting into the side of the hill as it turns westward. Notice the embankments. *Photo by author.*

began massaging his arms and legs and poured cold water on his chest. Their efforts were successful, and the lad eventually woke up, apparently none the worse for wear. There was one fatality, however. A man had been lying down not ten feet from Foster when the lighting hit. The man sat up, looked around curiously and then laid back down and died. Far from home, this veteran of countless battles and skirmishes was laid low not by a Minié ball but by a humble cloud.[71]

That evening, Hood issued orders to Stewart for the next day that would end the lives of hundreds of men as surely as the thunderbolt:

> *General Hood…desires that you will move against Big Shanty with your entire corps, and, should you be able to take possession of the place you can then send a division to Acworth. There are some rumors of there being as much as a division of the enemy at Marietta; you will therefore keep in constant communication with General Armstrong, who will advise you of any movement from the direction of Marietta. The report of this force at Marietta General Hood considers an additional reason for your moving on*

Big Shanty with your whole corps. General Hood thinks by Tuesday evening you had better draw back by your right flank toward Lost Mountain.

Here was Hood's big push. Instead of his whole army, as French advocated, one corps would march to the railroad, destroy it and return to Lost Mountain in two days.[72]

There was some justification for Hood's decision to reunite the army as quickly as possible. Sherman was far from idle. He had to decide whether to leave Atlanta and pursue the Confederates. For this, he relied on the results of his two infantry probes, as well as news from his cavalry north of the Chattahoochee. The division Howard sent to Fairburn reported Confederate cavalry and, erroneously, a corps of Rebel infantry still in the trenches near Palmetto. In truth, this was only a cavalry division guarding the rail line. East of the city, the division that Cox sent to Flat Rock found no enemy there. Instead, citizens informed them that what forces had been there had retired to Stockbridge or Jonesborough. He also marched a brigade of infantry to Stone Mountain and some cavalry to Lithonia. None encountered anything more than scouts.[73]

Sherman's cavalry was busy sending him information as well. Jennings's brigade of cavalry from Garrard's division had arrived during the early morning hours of the second. Upon arrival, they extended Kilpatrick's line north. In the morning, they would push out toward Powder Springs. McCook, with only about 170 cavalry on hand, was busy sending scouts in all directions. He reported enemy cavalry at Dallas.[74]

Sherman reached a decision. If Hood had two-thirds of his army north of the river, then he could attack the divided Confederates. Plus, he was already threatening Sherman's supply lifeline, so he could achieve two objectives: defeat Hood and safeguard the railroad. Orders were sent out by telegraph. He told Howard not to attack the "corps" still at Palmetto, as it was probably too entrenched. Instead, he directed Howard to have the division return from Fairburn and to prepare to move his army. Howard promptly got his men ready. He ordered his wagons to march for Atlanta the next day, and the infantry would follow after definitive word from Sherman. Sherman sent similar orders to Cox in Decatur: withdraw the division from Flat Rock and get ready to march your entire army to Atlanta at a moment's notice. On the other hand, Sherman ordered the Army of the Cumberland in Atlanta to begin moving immediately. It would march at first light on the next day.[75]

The Confederates were on the move as soon as dawn broke that Monday, October 3. However, they rarely saw the sun, as it rained throughout the night and continued to do so for the remainder of the day. While the rest of the army went northeast and ended its march at the Cooley House near Lost Mountain, Stewart's Corps went east toward the Western & Atlantic Railroad. Around noon, it passed through the remains of Lost Mountain Post Office, where "all the fences and every house save two or three had been burned." Armstrong's cavalry brigade joined it and covered the approaches from the south from the prying eyes of the Federals.[76]

The corps approached the railroad near the village of Big Shanty at about 5:00 p.m. in the afternoon. Armstrong's men turned south and occupied the former trenches the Federals had used to invest Kennesaw back in July. Their job was to halt or delay any reinforcements coming from the south. As his division neared the village, Loring deployed Featherston's Brigade in line of battle and sent it forward. Private Horace S. Lowry of the 14th and 15th Illinois Battalion was waiting for them. He and two others were manning a picket post on a hill west of town along the Acworth road. When two horsemen in gray appeared wearing the Texas star on their breasts, they leveled their rifles and fired. The cavalrymen beat a hasty retreat, and the gunfire brought out the rest of Companies A and B of the battalion. The men were instructed to be alert, and they did not have to wait long.

An enemy skirmish line soon emerged from the brush to their front, and the fighting began. Soon a solid line of battle, the remainder of Featherston's Brigade, came into view. The Federals beat a hasty retreat. Lowry delayed long enough to reload, and it almost cost him. Running the gauntlet of fire alone as he retreated, it was a miracle that none of the Rebel balls made contact. Several ladies stood on their piazzas, oblivious to the danger. Some wrung their hands and cried, while others of more secesh sympathies laughed and cheered the Rebels. The Illinoisans took refuge in the town's depot, which was surrounded by a platform. They had fortified it by piling rails on the platform along the building's outside walls and boring holes through the sides of the building. A short but violent firefight ensued. The Rebels got onto the platform, and when the Federals withdrew their rifle barrels after firing, they would insert their own weapons into the loopholes and fire inside. Soon the door was forced open, and the Illinoisans were compelled to surrender. The one hundred men of the garrison were marched into captivity. Walthall's Division went to Moon's Station about two miles north. After a brief fight over the stockade there that cost Reynold's Brigade six casualties, it captured an officer and eighty-three enlisted men from Company D.[77]

Loring's Division marched five miles northwest to Acworth. It arrived within one mile of the town and went into camp. The colonel of the 14th and 15th Illinois, George C. Rogers, was in Atlanta, leaving Captain Phineas D. Kenyon in command. With the three companies of the battalion already captured, this left only Companies C, K and E in Acworth. Rogers had left orders for Kenyon to take the battalion and fall back to Allatoona with all its supplies and baggage if attacked by a superior force. Unfortunately, Kenyon refused to believe that he was facing a superior force, even though Loring's campfires made a semicircle around the garrison. Kenyon believed that it was a cavalry ruse intended to scare them. He even forbade anyone from scouting the enemy and refused to move to Allatoona, against the advice of the remaining officers. Still, a few brave souls did go out to spy on the Confederates and reported back that it was a large force with artillery. Kenyon refused to budge. The three companies lay on their arms all night long awaiting an attack at dawn.

When Loring didn't attack at first light, Kenyon foolishly decided to take the battle to him. Bustling around "giving us orders as though the fate of a nation depended upon the issue," Kenyon advanced Companies C and K as skirmishers, leaving Company D as the reserve. Driving in the Rebel skirmishers, the Federals marched right into full view of the enemy camp. The Confederates were caught completely by surprise. Scrambling to get into formation, more than a few were laid low by the rifle fire of the Illinoisans. After forming, the Confederates charged with a yell. Foolish bravado aside, any chance the garrison had to escape evaporated. Fleeing headlong into the town, some took shelter in the depot, while others scattered among the few brick buildings that had been prepared for just such an attack. Corporal Lucius W. Barber of Company D scrambled atop an old store whose brick walls extended several feet above the roof. Several others from Company C joined him. They broke out bricks to make firing embrasures and shot at any Rebel who came within view.

Instead of launching a full-scale assault, Loring took his time. He let skirmishers engage the defenders, while he directed the rest of his division to surround the town. The encirclement complete, he deployed artillery that, according to Barber, "in fifteen minutes could level our defense to the earth, but with a reckless courage, we still fought on." Soon, however, a horseman rode forward waving a white flag. The firing ceased. Barber took the opportunity to return to his quarters, fill up his haversack and canteen and retrieve a box of hardtack. He was prepared for a siege on top of his brick building. On the way back, a furious shout rang out—they had been surrendered. Soon the garrison would join the rest of the unfortunate battalion on its way to Andersonville.[78]

The destruction of the railroad began immediately. French's men began tearing up the tracks at Big Shanty as soon as they arrived, and Loring and Walthall joined when they secured their respective objectives. French's Division moved north as it worked, Loring moved south and Walthall's men worked both ways until they met the others coming from either direction. The men went at it with a will. "To destroy is a soldier's joy," wrote Captain Joseph Boyce of the 1st and 4th Missouri:

Here was property belonging to our friends, but this was no concern of ours. The orders were to tear up the tracks, and at once the work was begun. Huge fires of ties were built, rails laid across them, the centre heated to a red heat, when they were carried over to the trees and bent until the ends met. In some cases the rails were twisted around the trunks of the trees forming a ring, and in every way possible destroying their usefulness. The corps worked throughout the night and into the next morning, tearing up tracks from Acworth to Big Shanty. Most did not get any rest. The men of Sears' Brigade were fortunate. They worked until 3 am, then were allowed a few hours of sleep, which they managed despite the rain. Afterwards, they went to work filling up a railroad cut near Big Shanty with whatever debris they could find, including logs, trees, stones, and dirt.[79]

The Union forces spent the third trying to find Hood's army. Major Jennings confirmed the presence of Hood near Lost Mountain, although ironically, Vandever's outpost on top of Kennesaw informed the cavalrymen first from its lofty perch. Kilpatrick's cavalry destroyed the bridge over Noyes Creek and moved north to reinforce Jennings. In the late morning, the Rebels cut the telegraph wires north of Marietta, severing communication north of the town. Still, before that happened, Sherman managed to inform Corse in Rome of the situation—that is, two of Hood's three corps were above the river, and Sherman was marching to intercept him. He also sent orders to Tourtellotte at Allatoona:

Hood has some infantry and cavalry about Powder Springs. I am watching him close. He might deceive us by his cavalry along Noyes Creek, and slip up to Acworth and Allatoona. I want the utmost vigilance there. If he goes for Allatoona I want him delayed only long enough for me to reach his rear. Of course his cavalry can only run across the road and bother us, but his infantry would try to capture stores, without which Hood cannot stay where he is. If he moves up toward Allatoona I will surely come in force.

The pass looking south through the gorge. The Star Fort is at the upper right. The footbridge would have been in the center. *Photo by author.*

Vandever informed Sherman that the Confederates had captured Big Shanty and were present in large numbers at Lost Mountain. Sherman responded by reminding Vandever that Marietta itself was of no value and to fall back to meet Stanley and the Army of the Cumberland should he be threatened. Or better yet, he should move to Kennesaw and fortify the summit.[80]

The Federals south of the Chattahoochee began the day as planned. The Army of the Cumberland moved out in the morning. The Fourth Corps left Atlanta and arrived at Smyrna Camp Ground north of the river at nightfall. The Fourteenth Corps followed and ended the day at the railroad bridge over the river. The Twentieth Corps, under Major General Henry W. Slocum, stayed behind to guard and hold the city. However, once the day started, Sherman began having second thoughts. He countermanded the march orders for Howard and Cox in the morning, and the two armies spent the day idling. Each, however, sent its baggage and supply trains ahead into Atlanta. In the evening, in light of the information coming in from north of the river and the cutting of the railroad, Sherman made up his mind. He issued definitive orders: at first light, the two armies were to move to Atlanta, cross the Chattahoochee and concentrate at Ruff's Station near Smyrna Camp Ground. He also sent a message to Kennesaw, to be signaled by Lieutenant Fish over the heads of Stewart's men via signal flag or torch. The message, directed to the commanding officers at Allatoona, Kingston and Rome, read: "The enemy is moving on Allatoona; thence to Rome." Unfortunately, a dense fog prevented the message from being relayed immediately. The warning would have to wait.[81]

Hood began the fourth by informing Cheatham and Lee that Stewart was on the railroad and destroying it. He ordered the two corps to strengthen their current position. He then decided to expand Stewart's mission of destruction. At 7:30 a.m., he dispatched an order to Stewart ordering him to move north:

> *General Hood directs that…you bring two of your divisions back…that your third division (say French's) shall move up the railroad and fill up the deep cut at Allatoona with logs, brush, rails, dirt, & c. To-morrow morning at daylight he desires…the division that will have gone to Allatoona to march thence to New Hope Church and on the position occupied by your other troops—that is, that the division shall rejoin your command by making this march out from the railroad and via New Hope. General Hood thinks that it is probable that the guard at the railroad bridge on Etowah is small, and when General French goes to Allatoona, if he can get such information as would justify him, if possible move to that bridge and destroy it. General Hood considers that its destruction would be a great advantage to the army and the country. Should he be able to destroy the bridge, in coming out he could move as has been heretofore indicted via New Hope.[82]*

Coincidentally, later in the morning, civilians alerted the officers in Stewart's Corps that the pass, four miles north of Acworth, was guarded by a far larger garrison than the outposts they had just captured. They told the Confederates that the pass had been fortified since it had been abandoned in May, was held by three and a half regiments and that it had become a large supply depot filled with provisions.

Stewart received the order at noon and immediately met with French. "General Hood does not seem to be aware that the place is fortified," he said, "and now, French, here is a fine opportunity for you."[83]

Shortly thereafter, they received a follow-up dispatch from Hood's staff, with even more detailed orders concerning the railroad bridge over the Etowah:

> *General Hood directs me to say that it is of the greatest importance to destroy the Etowah railroad bridge if such a thing is possible. From the best information we have now he thinks the enemy cannot disturb us before to-morrow, and by that time your main body will be near the remainder of our army. He suggests that if it is considered practicable to destroy the bridge when the division goes there and the artillery is placed in position, the commanding officer call for volunteers to go to the bridge with light wood and other combustible material that can he obtained and set fire to it.*[84]

The orders were quite specific and left very little to discretion. First, they specified French's Division as the one to take Allatoona. This was inopportune and unfortunate. French, at Big Shanty, was the farthest division from Allatoona. He was eight miles away from the pass, ten if they followed the railroad. Loring was already in Acworth, only four miles away by the most direct route, and his division was the largest in the corps. Even Walthall's Division at Moon's Station was closer. It would take a strong will and initiative to modify Hood's order based on the circumstances in the field. Stewart was a good officer and a competent corps commander. However, given the acrimonious end to the Atlanta Campaign, as well as Hardee's sacking less than a week earlier, it probably didn't seem wise or prudent to modify Hood's written order. Second, the order also specified the exact route on which French was to retire from Allatoona and reunite with the army. The purpose was to have French rejoin the army at Lost Mountain and have his division take its place on the defensive line with little confusion. However, the lack of discretion concerning this return route would have serious consequences in the future.

The orders were unfortunate in other aspects. After marching on the third, destroying the railroad during the night and next morning, French's men were expected to march to Allatoona, overpower its garrison and then fill in or obstruct the large railroad cut with whatever debris they could gather. Stewart and French now knew that there was a large garrison stationed there and behind new fortifications, something Hood did not know when he drafted the order. Even if they could get in position by the morning of the fifth, they would have been awake for more than forty-eight hours and then have to defeat the garrison and fill the cut. After all that was accomplished, it was strongly suggested that they move even farther north and destroy the bridge over the Etowah. That was a lot to expect from anybody.

Still, orders were orders, and the two generals set about fulfilling them as best they could. Stewart made preparations to move Loring and Walthall back to Lost Mountain. They would leave behind about eight miles of broken and useless track. He also helped bolster French's firepower. Currently, the division's artillery battalion contained only two batteries instead of the normal three: the Barbour Alabama Artillery under Captain Reuben Kolb and the Brookhaven Mississippi Artillery commanded by Captain James A. Hoskins. The battalion's commander, Major George W. Storrs, was absent, and Captain Kolb was temporarily in charge. Stewart assigned Major John D. Myrick to lead it and attached a battery from his battalion, the Pointe Coupée Louisiana Artillery, commanded by Lieutenant Ernest C. Legendre, to bring it up to strength.[85]

The fourth was a busy day for Sherman and his armies. Instead of sending Stanley north from Smyrna Camp Ground directly at Stewart, he ordered him west toward Little Kennesaw to guard the approaches from Lost Mountain. The Fourth Corps occupied the old Confederate works on the mountain at 5:30 p.m., and the Fourteenth ended the day slightly to the southwest at Nickajack Creek. By hard marching, Howard's Army of the Tennessee reached Smyrna Camp Ground in the evening, and Cox's Army of the Ohio made it across the Chattahoochee at Paces Ferry (ending the day near modern-day Vinings). Sherman, after issuing morning orders by telegraph, broke camp for his headquarters and moved north himself. He arrived at Smyrna Camp Ground that evening and had reestablished telegraphic communications with his units by at least 7:45 p.m.[86]

Once there, he immediately began issuing orders. First, he directed General Elliott to try and put a force of cavalry between Hood at Lost Mountain and Stewart on the railroad. He was, however, not to risk the safety of his cavalry until Sherman could arrive with the infantry. Instead, they were to make a bold reconnaissance and coordinate with Stanley. Garrard's Second Division marched north from Sweet Water, passed near Marietta, continued north of the mountain and there encountered Armstrong's cavalry manning the old Union trenches. Sherman also ordered Vandever to abandon Marietta, leave only a screen of fifty pickets to cover the town and move the rest of his men to the top of Kennesaw. Most importantly, he decided to concentrate the forces that were north of the Etowah. He directed General Corse in Rome to move his division to Cartersville and reinforce Smith's division, temporarily commanded by Brigadier General Green B. Raum.[87]

Fish and his signal station on top of Kennesaw were particularly busy that day. At first light, they were finally able to send the warning that had been delayed by fog.[88] At 9:30 a.m., they received a signal from Vandever in Marietta:

What do you observe this a.m.? Have you learned anything from Big Shanty?

Fish replied at 10:00 a.m.:

A large force of the enemy is hard at work burning the railroad both sides of Big Shanty.

At 2:00 p.m., Vandever had Fish relay a message to Tourtellotte at Allatoona:

Sherman is moving in force. Hold out.

This was followed up by another inquiry at 3:00 p.m.:

Have you communications by telegraph north?

The operator at Allatoona replied:

Yes; work as far as Kingston and Rome. The bridge at Resaca gone. Wheeler at Tilton yesterday after drove of cattle. Has partly destroyed track and wires.[89]

During the afternoon, Sherman's orders to Corse went over the heads of the Rebels via Fish:

Sherman directs you to move forward and join Smith's division with your entire command, using cars, if to be had, and burn provisions rather than lose them.[90]

Finally, Sherman had the station on top of Kennesaw send a direct message for Corse to move to Allatoona:

Move your command to Allatoona. Hold the place. I will help you.

General Vandever sent the final word of encouragement by signal to Allatoona at 6:30 p.m.:

General Sherman says hold fast. We are coming.[91]

After spending the morning filling in the railroad cuts around Big Shanty, French's weary soldiers fell into formation and received their marching orders at about three o'clock. The smoke from the myriad fires hung in the air as the men began their journey north. They didn't know it, but they were in a race. And Allatoona was the prize.[92]

Chapter 8

I Will Pitch Into Them

Rome, Georgia, was a quiet little Southern town. It rested at the confluence of the Etowah and Oostanaula Rivers, which joined to form the Coosa River. It was a regional crossroads and was connected to the Western & Atlantic Railroad by its own spur line, the Rome Railroad. The town was also a center of industry, most notably the Noble & Co. Ironworks and Machine Shop. Abel Streight and his Union raiders had been captured nearby in 1863, prompting the fortification of the town. It was captured early in the Atlanta Campaign the following year, ironically after being briefly defended by French's Division. Now it was a supply base for the Union army, defended by the division commanded by Brigadier General John M. Corse.[93]

Born in 1835 in Pittsburg, Pennsylvania, Corse was raised in Burlington, Iowa, where his father served six terms as mayor. He attended West Point for two years but did not graduate, and he was admitted to the Iowa bar. In 1860, he was the state's Democratic nominee for secretary of state. When war broke out, he was elected major of the 6th Iowa Infantry. He was adept at both staff and field command. Early in the war, he served on the staff of General John Pope during his Mississippi Campaign, and he served valiantly at the head of the 6th Iowa at Corinth and Vicksburg. Promoted to brigadier general in August 1863, he was wounded leading his brigade on Missionary Ridge. He returned to duty as Sherman's inspector general for the Atlanta Campaign, another staff job, but was given command of Sweeney's old division in late July. This became the Fourth Division of the Fifteenth Corps after the September reorganization.[94]

John M. Corse, after promotion to major general. *Library of Congress, LC-BH83-2242.*

Corse was a strict disciplinarian, and his men certainly appreciated it and respected him for it, but it appears that they didn't particularly like him. The postwar history of the 6th Iowa is notably absent of any actual praise for him. In fact, Corse was the type of officer who was not above saying one thing and then changing his mind if the outcome failed to suit him. Anyone who has served in the military would probably recognize the type. Near the end of one particularly grueling march in Mississippi, the 6th Iowa stopped at a town just short of its camp. Colonel Corse, commanding the regiment at the time, addressed the men. "Those who feel that they are not able to march the rest of the distance to camp step four paces to the front," he asked. He was expecting his men to be hard-core and volunteer to march the rest of the way. However, two officers and a number of men stepped forward. An exasperated Corse made them get back in line and declared that the unfortunates would walk the rest of the way to camp if it took three days. He was true to his word. While following the rail line on their march, a freight train approached and stopped for them. Corse allowed everyone to board except those who had stepped out of line. The balance of the regiment took the train the remaining distance to the camp. The "cripple" squad arrived the next morning, on foot. In short, John Corse was a bit of a jerk.[95]

Not everyone had such a low opinion of Corse, though. Captain Ludlow thought him "active and alert, ambitious, combative, decided, of sound judgment and indomitable courage." Grant would later write in his memoirs, "Corse was a man who would never surrender."[96]

Sherman had sent Corse to Rome to protect the town, as well as the railroad bridge over the Tennessee River at Bridgeport, Alabama, against any Confederate thrust from Gadsden. He had also given Corse verbal orders to be "ready at all times to strike in any direction the enemy might be discovered taking." He immediately sealed the city and surrounding areas to civilian traffic, began improving the existing forts surrounding the town and had the men build new earthworks where necessary. He began drilling, organizing and getting the division ready as a rapid-response force. With two mounted regiments at his disposal, he sent scouts in all directions to gather information about the enemy. After the Confederates cut the railroad, however, Sherman sent the signal over the heads of the Rebels ordering Corse to link up with Raum at Cartersville.[97]

General Raum had been busy at Cartersville as well. General Smith had earlier gone to Chattanooga to coordinate the forwarding of supplies south, leaving Raum in charge of the division. In a creative act of espionage, on October 2, Raum sent the wife of an unwilling Confederate recruit into Hood's camp on the pretext of seeing her husband. They were both Union sympathizers, but public pressure had forced him to enlist in the service. Once there, she gathered as much information as possible, returning at about noon on the fourth with news of the Confederate advance. Guessing that Allatoona would be next, Raum warned Tourtellotte and requested that Corse move directly to the pass instead of stopping at Cartersville.[98]

Getting to Allatoona was easier said than done. With the bridge at Resaca gone and the line cut at Acworth, the only engines and cars available were those that happened to be trapped between those two points. To top it off, there was a derailment between Kingston and Rome, blocking the line. Raum summoned Captain George W. Hill of his staff and gave him the following order:

> *Proceed with the engine to Rome and hand to General Corse the enclosed letter.*
> *I learn that two cars must be put on the track before you can reach Rome.*
> *Have as little delay as possible; throw the cars off, if that is the most expeditious way of disposing of them.*
> *Moments are of importance, so improve them.*

Hill went to work with a will. Taking with him four soldiers and two railroad employees, he boarded an engine and made for Kingston. Unfortunately, the engineer running the engine was less than reliable. Although ordered to go as fast as possible, the man would only move down the line about as fast as a person could walk. When asked, the engineer replied that would not go any faster because he wanted to be able to jump and run if the Johnnies surprised them, as he had no intention of being sent south as a prisoner. After calling the soldiers to the engine, Hill put his hand on the man's shoulder. "You run this engine as fast as possible, or I will throw you off and go on without you. You are not necessary, we can go without you." The engineer took the hint, and soon they were barreling down the rails to make up lost time.

At Kingston, they appropriated twelve cars and started for Rome. About eight miles out, they ran into the blockage. Two hospital cars loaded with supplies had derailed because a boulder had fallen onto the track, disabling it. The car's engine had continued to Rome to fill its boiler with water, and a gang of railroad workers was trying to right the cars. Captain Hill ordered the hospital cars pitched over an embankment to get them out of the way. They were also able to remove the boulder from the tracks. The section foreman assured Hill that the line would be repaired in about an hour. Telling the engineer in their car to follow them to Rome as soon as the track was repaired, Hill and his companions continued in a handcar. They met the hospital car's engine coming the other way, and Hill rode it to the break, sending the handcar to Rome. True to his word, at the break the foreman was just finishing the last repairs; the line was opened. The two engines and tenders raced to Rome. Hill rode with the new engineer, and unlike the previous one, he entered into the spirit of Hill's orders with enthusiasm. Together with the cars from Kingston, he agreed to have a train of twenty cars prepared once they arrived, with an engine at both ends. They arrive at sunset.

Hill immediately went to Corse's headquarters. He found him resting on a cot and handed the general the dispatch. After reading it, Corse told Hill, "I can't get to Allatoona, the road is all torn up."

"Oh, no, general, the road is all right, I have just come over it with an engine and 'tis repaired."

"I have had one brigade in line all day waiting to go, but I can't get control of the damned railroad, and I have just ordered them to camp again, and given up going," replied Corse.

"I have control of a train for you," said Hill, "with two engines and twenty cars, and can load you in twenty minutes if you will have your men at the depot."

"You can't get a train when I can't," replied Corse quickly.

"But, I say to you, I have what I tell you, twenty cars and two engines."

"How the hell could you get a train when I could not?"

"I just took control, that is all there is to it," finished Hill. After ordering his division to the depot, Corse asked him what he might expect. Hill gave him what information he could and noted that Corse would get all the fight he wanted.

"If I go down there I will pitch into them by God, if there is thirty thousand."[99]

At the moment, that horde of "thirty thousand" was in Acworth. Like Hill at Rome, the soldiers arrived there as the sun was setting. They paused for two reasons. First, the men had to wait for the commissaries to issue rations. Second, French needed to secure the services of a local guide to show them the way to Allatoona in the dark. He was able to find a young boy who knew the local roads and had seen the fortifications, as he was a member of a cavalry company. He also interviewed two young ladies who had visited Allatoona just that afternoon. They gave him Tourtellotte's name, as well as their best guess at the garrison's strength. French gave Captain Taylor and twenty-five men from the 1st Mississippi Cavalry of Armstrong's Brigade the job of riding north of Allatoona and taking up rails from the track. That would prevent or delay any reinforcements arriving from north of the Etowah. From high ground nearby, French could see torch signals being used to communicate between Allatoona and Kennesaw, as well as Federal campfires to the south and east, most likely Garrard's cavalry. He would have to keep them in mind. He couldn't waste any more time and risk being cut off from the main army at Lost Mountain.[100]

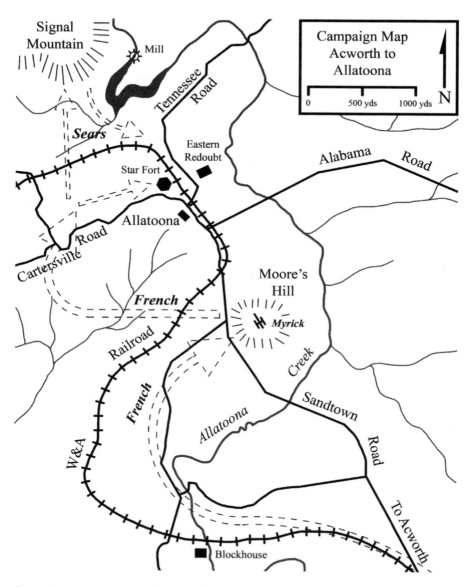

Campaign map Acworth to Allatoona. *Courtesy of the author.*

The march to Allatoona began at 11:00 p.m. There were two routes to Allatoona: the direct road to the east and the railroad to the west. French chose to follow the railroad. Skirmishers, thin lines of soldiers spaced several yards apart, spread out from the marching column in all directions. They protected those marching from being surprised, gave an early warning when contact with the enemy was initiated and scouted the enemy when possible. After about three miles, the column reached the railroad bridge over Allatoona Creek, guarded by three companies of the 18th Wisconsin. Destroying the bridge was important, but French didn't have time to invest the blockhouse and force its surrender. He left behind the 4th Mississippi and one cannon to try and capture the blockhouse if possible. With the rest of the division, he continued on.

To the east, French's skirmishers closed up on Allatoona Creek near the road crossing. Here the 18th Wisconsin had a thin line of pickets on watch—Company B under Captain Thomas A. Jackson. Jackson's men had dismantled the road bridge earlier in the day and were keeping watch to the south. The Rebel pickets were only about twenty yards away on the other side of the creek, but for the moment, they had not attempted to cross to their side. They could plainly hear the rumble of wagons and the yelling of mule drivers upstream to their right. Realizing that they were outflanked, Jackson quietly removed his company from its position and moved it up the hill behind them.

At the top, the terrain leveled out. To the south, the direction they retreated from, the hillside sloped down to the road bridge over the creek. To the southeast, a ridge paralleled the creek below. The railroad followed this ridge, as did another road leading to a nearby ford. To the north, a wide, open saddle containing the depot and Allatoona village connected this ridge with the elevation containing the railroad pass. The railroad and several roads converged at the elevated area where Jackson regrouped, and nearby stood an old, dilapidated house. To the east of the road, there was a low, open hill named Moore's Hill.

At the crossroads, Jackson's company met a sergeant and eight men from Company A whose orders were to scout out the main road. They were to fire into anybody or anything that did not promptly answer the challenge. They made it fifty yards before they ran headlong into two companies of Texans. The Wisconsin men immediately opened fire—the first shots of the Battle of Allatoona Pass. The Texans responded in kind, and the Confederates had the advantage of numbers. The Rebels soon pushed them away from the crossroads and back down to their main skirmish line closer to the village.[101]

Looking east into the entrance to the Eastern Redoubt. *Photo by author.*

With the intersection cleared, the head of French's Division pulled up at about 3:00 a.m. It was pitch black, and French could see nothing except a few twinkling lights on the ridge to the north. The guide told him that the cleared area around Moore's Hill was a good place for the artillery, so French ordered Major Myrick to deploy there as best he could, facing the heights across the saddle. From that position, the forts were about 1,200 yards away. To protect the artillery, French ordered the 39th North Carolina and 32nd Texas from Ector's Brigade to stay and support them.[102]

Now the Confederate commander had to make a choice. He had to storm the pass, but from which direction? If he moved straight ahead, he would be charging into the combined firepower of both forts and their supporting infantry. Not an attractive option. His other choice was to flank the position and attack along the ridge, where he would only be subjected to fire from one fort at a time. But which direction? To the right was Allatoona Creek, an all but impenetrable barrier in the dead of night. It would certainly impede any attempt to move across and around it, and keeping his division together while doing so at night would slow down the advance. The only realistic choice was to move to the left, or west, and approach the pass from that direction.

There were no roads that could take them in that direction except the Cartersville Road. Unfortunately, the road ran straight north into the village, up the hill under the very teeth of the Star Fort and then followed the ridge west. So the guide took them down off the ridge near Moore's Hill, oriented as best he could to the west, and plunged into the dark woods. The column of infantry followed. Down the side of the ridge they went and then up and down numerous draws and gullies. Before long, the young guide had to admit that he was hopelessly lost. Instead of continuing to march through the forest in the hopes of somehow gaining the ridge to the north, French made a prudent decision. He called a halt. The men could rest until dawn. They would wait until daylight allowed them to orient themselves and deploy to their advantage. Gratefully, the men fell out of the ranks and were quickly asleep.[103]

Back at Rome, Corse was busy loading as much of his division on the train as the twenty cars would hold. He was able to cram on board his Third Brigade, led by Colonel Richard Rowett. The brigade contained the 7th, 50th and 57th Illinois, as well as the 39th Iowa. They were tough veterans who had fought at Fort Donelson, Shiloh and Corinth. They had spent most of 1863 guarding northern Alabama from cavalry raids. While the 7th had been detached, the other three marched with Sherman from Chattanooga and fought at Resaca in May. At the end of that month, the brigade was assigned to garrison Rome, where it had been ever since. As they boarded the train, all were understrength. They still had companies out on the skirmish lines of the forts and earthworks or detached to garrison the town itself. The nine companies of the 7th had about 313 officers and men, the eight companies of the 50th had 267 and the eight companies of the 39th loaded 284. Only two companies of the 57th made it on board, with 66 men. Also crammed on the train was a detachment of the 12th Illinois from the Second Brigade, numbering 163. With staff, including engineers such as Lieutenant William Ludlow, approximately 1,093 officers and men were rushing to save the garrison at Allatoona that night.[104]

Their commander, Richard Rowett, had only recently taken over command of the brigade. He began the war as captain of Company K, 7th Illinois. When that regiment reenlisted after its initial three months of service expired, he was elected major. He received high praise for his performance at Fort Donelson:

Enthusiastic, but not rash, he was found where all the brave were found. None but could admire his dash so free, so courageous as he moved with the regiment on those hills with defiance, lacing danger and cheering his men on to victory. Says he, since the battle: "I never felt so happy in all my life as when before that rebel battery the first day; happy because I there discovered that I had a heart to face the cannon's mouth, which I did not feel certain of having until then."

Wounded at Shiloh, he fought valiantly at Corinth. He rose to the head of the regiment in February 1863 and was elevated to brigade command on August 15, 1864.[105]

One regiment boarded the train feeling particularly confident. Almost all of the 7th Illinois were armed with the Henry repeating rifle. Most of the infantry in both armies carried single-shot muzzle-loading rifles, such as the 1861 Springfield or the 1853 British Enfield. Soldiers could fire three rounds per minute, although in the stress and excitement of combat, this could vary wildly. The lever-action Henry carried sixteen rounds in a tube magazine. After firing one round, reloading was as easy as operating the lever underneath the receiver. Reloading an empty tube took a little longer, but the volume of fire available to the shooter in a short period of time was tremendous. One disadvantage of the rifle was that the bullet fired was little more than an oversized pistol round, which severely hampered the range. Still, at less than one hundred yards, the amount of lead it could send downrange helped alleviate this shortcoming.

The Henry rifles had a strange journey into the hands of the 7th. During the summer, Captain John A. Smith of Company E had tried to secure orders allowing him to travel to the Henry factory in Hartford, Connecticut, but was denied. He then secured a leave of absence and traveled north at his own expense. When he got to Hartford, he found that while the factory had no inventory at that moment, five hundred of them had been shipped to Chicago. He telegraphed Chicago to hold the rifles and left on the first train. Once there, he found out that he would have to pay $52.50 for each rifle instead of $47.50. He paid the difference out of his own pocket and sent them south by express. During a stopover in Cincinnati, he noticed boxes being unloaded into a warehouse. They were marked "Captain J.A. Smith, 7th Illinois Infantry." When he asked why they were being stored, he was told that no express shipments were to go south unless they were prepaid. He had to borrow money from a friend to prepay the freight. When they arrived in Georgia a few days before, the regiment purchased the entire shipment.

Considering enlisted men were paid $13.00 a month, this was three months' pay—quite an investment. Among the unpacked rifles was a silver-plated specimen, engraved with Captain Smith's name, a gift from the Chicago agent who helped broker the deal. The 7th Illinois boarded the train with a distinct firepower advantage.[106]

By 8:30 p.m., everyone and everything had been loaded, including an extra 165,000 rounds of ammunition. After agreeing on a set of signals to give in case of danger or an accident, Hill and Corse boarded the train. Hill rode in the front engine. Despite all the preparations, the ride went smoothly and without incident. Captain Taylor's company of the 1st Mississippi Cavalry never appeared below the Etowah and did nothing to damage the track or delay the train. At 1:00 a.m., the train rounded a curve, and the earth appeared to swallow the tracks in the dark night as they entered the deep cut. Emerging on the other side, the engines came to a halt at the depot on the other side. French and his division were still miles away, probably near the bridge and blockhouse. Corse had won the race. Now he would have to fight to keep the prize.[107]

Chapter 9

A Needless Effusion of Blood

While the night was dark, especially for French's infantry wandering around lost in the woods, it was not without its ambiance. To the garrison high on the ridge, "the campfires of the enemy and the flames of burning railroad ties cast red light through all the forests and hills and valleys between Allatoona and Big Shanty, tinged the clouds with bright colors, and, at times, clearly disclosed the rugged outlines of Kennesaw Mountain, eighteen miles away." Into this surreal environment the men of Rowett's brigade disembarked from the train.[108]

As soon as they were off, they assembled in the open fields east of the village. The 50th Illinois had its right anchored on the railroad embankment, and the 12th Illinois formed on the left. The 7th Illinois deployed behind it. The companies of the 57th Illinois also lay down to relax, but the regiment's location was not recorded. The men were ordered to stack arms, and they rested as best they could. Quite a few fell asleep, but they didn't rest long. Fighting started to the south about half an hour later. Captain Mortimer R. Flint, a member of Corse's staff, tried to get some sleep under a nearby clump of trees. However, "owing to the careless manner in which the enemy handled their firearms, bullets from them forced their way among us in an unseemly hurried manner, zipping through the trees and occasionally striking the ground near us." Unable to sleep, and thinking of a way to make his mark on history to his own advantage, Flint went to Corse and suggested moving the ammunition from the depot's platform to the Star Fort. Corse agreed, and soon the two companies of the 57th Illinois were lugging the wooden ammunition crates up the hill.[109]

Orders came to form the regiments into a defensive position. The 7th Illinois moved briefly about two hundred yards ahead and then crossed over to the other side of the tracks. It formed in line of battle with its left resting on the embankment. The 50th fell back slightly from its former position and into line on its left, with the 12th behind it in reserve. The men of the 50th created a hasty barricade by overturning army wagons in front of their position. They were in column of divisions, a formation intended not for battle but rather for ease of maneuvering. Shortly after dawn, they were ordered to the top of the hill and fell in beside the 4th Minnesota in the earthworks on the northern crest. The 57th Illinois redeployed to the Star Fort. The exact whereabouts of the 39th Iowa during the night is unknown. However, at dawn, it was ordered into line about two hundred yards west of the depot to cover that flank, but as soon as it formed, it was again ordered west to occupy the strong redoubt astride the Cartersville Road.[110]

Of the garrison, the 472 men of the 4th Minnesota held the ridge east of the railroad, including the Eastern Redoubt. Company E under Captain Daniel G. Towle was sent out into the darkness to form a skirmish line north of the railroad. Companies A and I held the small U-shaped half-fort just above and to the east of the cut. The 93rd Illinois, 294 officers and men strong but spread out, filled the Star Fort and the works to the west. Three companies manned the rifle pits around the Star Fort. Two companies were in the fort itself. Five companies under the control of the regimental commander, Major James M. Fisher, were several hundred yards in front of the redoubt on the Cartersville Road. Centered on the two old redoubts, they covering the approaches from the west. The six cannons of the 12th Wisconsin Battery were equally divided between the two forts. Two three-inch rifles and one twelve-pounder Napoleon were in the Star Fort, and the other half of the battery was in the Eastern Redoubt. The battery's commander, Captain William Zickerick, was in Cartersville. While he was away, the cannoneers were being led by Lieutenant Marcus Amsden. When the fighting broke out near Moore's Hill, Lieutenant Colonel Charles H. Jackson (brother of Captain Jackson of Company B), commanding the regiment, ordered the 18th Wisconsin forward. There, the 156 men of the remaining seven companies established a long skirmish line south of the pass and sparred with the Texans and North Carolinians on Moore's Hill.[111]

Dawn broke on Wednesday the fifth, "calm and clear, with the crisp air and bright warm sun of that superb mountain region," according to

Lieutenant Ludlow. Not long after the sun rose, when the light was good enough to see, Major Myrick gave the signal for his battalion to open fire on the two forts. It was about 6:30 a.m. or 7:00 a.m. His orders were to continue firing until the assaulting Confederate lines drew close to the fort and the danger of hitting their own men was too great. The earth shook beneath their feet as eleven cannons roared to life. Unfortunately, the range was just too great. The bombardment did inflict some casualties but, on the whole, not many. Most of the shots went wild and did very little damage. They did, however, kill twenty-seven of the horses belonging to the 12th Wisconsin Battery. The Wisconsin men responded in kind. One round fired by Lieutenant Samuel E. Jones in the Eastern Redoubt dismounted a Rebel cannon, and the hills echoed with the cheers of the onlooking infantry. With that, the Confederate gunners moved their pieces back to the cover of woods at the crest of Moore's Hill and continued the bombardment from what little cover it provided.[112]

When the cannonade started, the skirmishing south of the pass intensified. It was obvious that the regiments stationed below the fort were much too exposed. Colonel Rowett ordered the 12th Illinois under Captain Robert Koehler up the hill to report to, and apparently take orders from, Lieutenant Colonel William Hana of the 50th Illinois. To avoid the cannonade, they filed through the railroad cut and ascended the hill from the sheltered north side. Once at the top, they leapt into the earthworks alongside the 50th. Colonel Rowett told Lieutenant Colonel Hector Perrin of the 7th Illinois to send two companies farther south to reinforce the 18th Wisconsin and join the 39th Iowa in the redoubt along the Cartersville Road. Selecting Companies E and H for skirmish duty, and another to cover their withdrawal if necessary, Perrin moved the remaining six northwest.

Once there, the regiment took its place alongside the 39th Iowa. Its right rested on the road, with the regiment facing south. The 39th Iowa held the trenches north of the road facing west. Companies B and C were out front skirmishing alongside the five of the 93rd Illinois. Companies A, F and I were outside the redoubt in support, "sent forward 300 yards to the right and front of the main line to hold the crest of a hill." This placed them on the next ridge to the west. Only the remaining three companies, E, G and K, were stationed in the redoubt itself. The two companies of the 57th Illinois were deployed as skirmishers somewhere outside the Star Fort, possibly along the ridges north of the redoubt. The little fort also received a welcome boost in firepower. The twelve-pounder Napoleon smoothbore from the Star Fort was taken out and dragged forward. It was placed in the bastion on the high

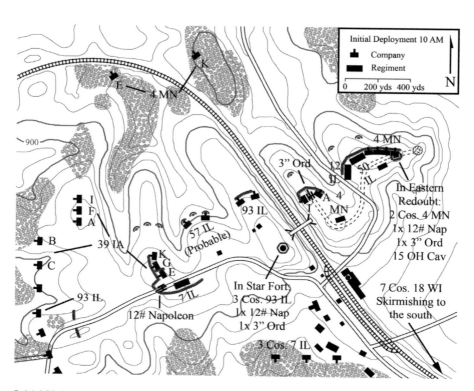

Initial Union deployment. Unit sizes are not to scale. *Courtesy of the author.*

ground at the Cartersville Road, at or near the apex of the angle formed by the two wings of the redoubt. Colonel Tourtellotte also redeployed some of his artillery. He had one of the three-inch ordnance rifles moved from the Eastern Redoubt to the small redoubt sheltering Companies A and I of the 4th Minnesota, overlooking the railroad cut.[113]

General French had his men up and moving as soon as it was light enough to see. "The day dawned beautiful and bright," he later wrote, "and as the sun rose higher and higher in the mellow autumnal sky, and lit up the forest-clad heights, it turned into a quiet Indian summer day of hazy, drowsy appearance inducive of rest." But there would be no rest that day. As they made their way through the gullies and hills, they heard the bombardment begin to their right. The men trudged north until they crested the ridge at about 7:30 a.m. Once on high ground, in daylight, they got their first look at the Union fortifications. Lieutenant George W. Warren of the 3rd and 5th Missouri observed the scene with a veteran's eye. "As I looked across the intervening space to the bristling forts and viewed the rugged mountain side with the interminable abatis that lay between, and then cast my eyes along our slender line, I thought to myself there will be hot work here if those regiments are made up of resolute men."[114]

French quickly fashioned a plan of attack. He determined to make the assault from both flank and rear in a classic pincer. He swiftly began deploying Cockrell and Ector's Brigades along the crest of the ridge facing east. They would traverse the crest, capture the redoubt at the Cartersville Road and then assault the Star Fort. While Cockrell and Young formed the anvil, Sears' Brigade would attack from the north. Between the two, they could outflank the defenders and pry them from their reviled earthworks. Accordingly, French ordered Sears to continue marching north. Once he was directly north of, and even east of, the railroad and Star Fort, his orders were to deploy in line of battle and attack. However, with the two wings out of sight, coordination would be difficult. Therefore, French resolved to have Cockrell and Young wait until they heard firing from the north, signaling that Sears had commenced his attack. That way they would know he was in position. Once they heard the shooting start, French would order Cockrell and Young to move out.[115]

The march from the Chattahoochee, burning the railroad at Big Shanty and the night march to Allatoona without any appreciable sleep all whittled away at the strength of the division. In all likelihood, stragglers and deserters were left along the line of march from the Moon House at Lost Mountain to the draws and gullies below Moore's Hill. Keeping in mind the 4th Mississippi at the blockhouse, as well as the two regiments supporting the artillery at Moore's Hill, French estimated that he had "but little over two thousand men." Cockrell's Brigade had 1,050 men poised for the attack. Ector's Brigade had about 400. This left Sears' Brigade with approximately of 700 to 800 infantrymen. Even if French was underreporting the force available as enlisted men only, the total wouldn't increase much. Individual regiments were skeletons of their former selves. Most numbered between 100 and 200 strong. Many had less than 100. Adding in the officers, if they weren't already included in French's total, would probably only increase the total by another 100 or so. It would be a hard fight. The infantry at French's disposal roughly equaled the men Corse had in the garrison, and the defenders were behind stout forts and earth fortifications. Not good odds for an assault. French would have to bring more forces to bear at one section of the enemy's line and hope to overwhelm the strong points individually.[116]

Sears's flanking march immediately went awry. He first headed almost due north and paused on the southeastern slope of Signal Mountain, high ground whose peak is about two thousand yards northwest of the Star Fort. He intended to move directly southeast toward the Union position, but Allatoona Creek presented an unforeseen obstacle. The creek formed a sharp curve pointing southwest. The federal soldiers at the garrison had raised the height of a milldam upstream, with the result that the creek was flooded and not easily fordable. Sears sent French a note, along with a quick sketch of his position, explaining his difficulty:

> *I have a very difficult position to deploy upon; am sending out my skirmishers and they have commenced firing, but few are in position. Am crowding them forward; have to debouch around the bend in the bayou. I will form line of battle as soon as I can drive their skirmish line far enough back, and will push the matter as far as the honor of our arms may seem to demand.*

It would take more time to "debouch around the bend in the bayou," as Sears put it, and he was not doing so unopposed. His skirmishers ran into Captain Towle and his Company E. It was an unequal match, and Towle sent back to Tourtellotte for help. Soon Company K, led by Captain Ira N. Morrill, was rushing forward to support him. Morrill deployed his company east of the railroad. The Rebels on the mountainside ahead were plainly visible, and the tracks disappeared into the cut to his left.[117]

An officer remarked near William Chambers of the 46th Mississippi that taking the place was "only a breakfast task." Chambers, feeling that the mission before them was a more serious undertaking than others were predicting, told the officer that "anybody was welcome to my share of that breakfast."[118]

It was past nine o'clock, and French impatiently waited for Sears. To the east, the fire from his artillery slackened and then ceased. French was still under the impression that the garrison ahead contained only three regiments. Perhaps realizing that they were outnumbered, French could appeal to their common sense and stop the attack before it began. He wrote out a note and handed it to his adjutant, Major David W. Sanders. French instructed him to carry the message to the Union lines under a flag of truce and wait for about seventeen minutes for a response. Major Sanders rode east along the Cartersville Road, accompanied by Assistant Inspector General E.T. Freeman and a detachment of sixteen men from the 29th North Carolina.[119]

They soon encountered the skirmish line of the 93rd Illinois on the Cartersville Road. After halting, Major Sanders handed the note to Lieutenant William C. Kinney, who immediately carried it eastward. He encountered Colonel Rowett at the redoubt to the east. Rowett, after searching, found Corse and Tourtellotte near the Star Fort. Corse opened the note and read it:

Around Allatoona, October 5, 1864.
COMMANDING OFFICER U.S. FORCES, Allatoona:

SIR: I have placed the forces under my command in such position that you are surrounded, and to avoid a needless effusion of blood, I call on you to surrender your forces at once and unconditionally. Five minutes will be allowed you to decide. Should you accede to this, you will be treated in the most honorable manner as prisoners of war.

I have the honor to be, very respectfully, yours,
S.G. FRENCH,
Major-General, Commanding C.S. Forces.

Corse immediately dismounted, sat down on a stump and composed a reply:

HEADQUARTERS FOURTH DIVISION, FIFTEENTH ARMY CORPS,
Allatoona, Ga., October 5, 1864—8.30 a.m.
Maj. Gen. S.G. FRENCH, C.S. Army, &c.:

Your communication demanding surrender of my command I acknowledge receipt of, and would respectfully reply that we are prepared for the "needless effusion of blood" whenever it is agreeable to you.

I am, very respectfully, your obedient servant,
JNO. M. CORSE,
Brigadier-General, Commanding U.S. Forces.

Private Elisha Starbuck of the 39th Iowa was nearby and witnessed Corse write the reply. Corse handed the note to Lieutenant Oliver C. Ayers of the 39th Iowa. "They will now be upon us," Corse remarked to Tourtellotte. Ayers and Starbuck took off down the slope toward the awaiting major. As they passed the redoubt at the Cartersville Road,

Ayers and Starbuck parted ways. Starbuck rejoined the 39th, and Ayers continued on to Major Sanders.[120]

Out on the skirmish line, Captain Morrill of the 4th Minnesota watched tensely as Sears's men descended the slopes of Signal Mountain and made their way forward around the bend in Allatoona Creek. Shortly afterward, an officer in gray approached him with a white handkerchief tied to his sword.

"Do you not know that there has been a flag of truce sent in to your commanding officer demanding your surrender?" he asked. The single star on his collar identified him as a major.

"No," replied Morrill. "What do you want? Do you want to surrender?"

"I do not," said the major.

"Well, then you had better drop down out of sight, as my boys were not feeling very friendly toward you."

While talking to the major, Morrill noticed that the Rebel brigade behind him was still moving. If there was a temporary truce, the enemy was certainly violating it by advancing to obtain a better position without the threat of being shot. The captain sent out two men, one in each direction. They came back quickly and breathlessly told Morrill that they were being surrounded. Shouting, "Boys, follow me!" he led them back to the main line, or as he put it, "We made the home-stretch in pretty fair time."[121]

Back at the 93rd Illinois' skirmish line, Major Sanders waited impatiently for the reply. The note had specified that the Yanks had five minutes to respond, and French had told him seventeen minutes. Sanders had waited twenty. Feeling that there was no answer forthcoming, Sanders turned his horse west and led his party away from the rifle pits and back into their lines.[122]

Whether Corse answered French's ultimatum became a source of controversy after the war. In both his contemporary diary and in his official report written only one month after the battle, French always maintained that he never received a reply. Sanders himself, in a letter written to French decades after the war, confirmed that he never received an answer to the ultimatum, even after waiting twenty minutes. On the other hand, Corse adamantly insisted that he did write out an answer. He even went so far as to include the text of French's original ultimatum, and his reply, in his official report. Colonel Tourtellotte and Private Starbuck both witnessed Corse writing the note, and Starbuck accompanied Lieutenant Ayers as far as the redoubt along the Cartersville Road. However, he did not actually witness it being handed over to any Confederate.[123]

This raises several questions. Was Corse's reply actually delivered? Did Lieutenant Ayers arrive to find that Major Sanders had already departed? Did the lieutenant hand the reply to somebody other than the major, and the note was not sent up the chain of command? The latter is certainly a possibility. Another possibility is that Lieutenant Ayers arrived to find that the Rebel party had left and returned to Corse with the reply undelivered. Corse never mentioned this, naturally. However, this brings up even more questions. How did Corse preserve the exact text of his reply? With time of the essence, did he write out two exact copies of his response as he sat in the hot sun on a tree stump? One to give to Major Sanders and one to preserve for posterity? Did he write down another, perhaps inexact, copy from memory later on? Ayers would perish in less than an hour. Did somebody go through his personal effects and return the note to Corse, who then pocketed it for future reference? We may never know for sure. What is certain is that combat was imminent.

As Sanders rode back through his lines, a Missourian called out to him, "Is it surrender or fight, Major?" His concise reply was both electrifying and dreadful.

"Fight!"[124]

Chapter 10

The Bayonet Was Freely Used

The Confederates formed under the warm morning sun into two lines of battle. In the forefront, Cockrell's Missourians lined up for the task ahead. The 1st and 3rd Missouri were on the right, followed on the left by the 3rd and 5th, the 1st and 4th and, finally, the 2nd and 6th. The brigade was centered on the ridge, with skirmishers deployed ahead to lead the advance and screen the division. Officers told the men to throw off everything but their cartridge and cap boxes, and the command "load at will" echoed down the line. To add to the tension, Major William F. Carter of the 2nd and 6th Missouri walked among the men and passed along the order to take no prisoners. The upcoming assault promised to be grim indeed. Behind them and aligned slightly to the left, the Texans and North Carolinians of Ector's Brigade formed up to support Cockrell, if necessary. From right to left were the 9th Texas, 14th Texas Cavalry and 10th Texas Cavalry. The 29th North Carolina completed the brigade line on the left. It extended past the left of the 2nd and 6th Missouri ahead of them. Between the two brigades, there were 1,450 Confederates ready to go. They would be facing about 742 men of 7th Illinois, 93rd Illinois and 39th Iowa, both in the redoubt and on the skirmish line. However, this number included the three companies of the 7th skirmishing below the village, so they had even fewer available in the trench. Still, at the point of attack, French had stacked the odds two to one in his favor.[125]

To the east, Corse was making preparations of his own. As soon as Lieutenant Ayers left, he turned to Colonel Tourtellotte and ordered him to take command of all the forces on the east side of the railroad tracks. Tourtellotte immediately left his command. Corse then told Rowett to take charge of the two regiments in the redoubt to the west. He then personally accompanied two companies of the 93rd Illinois and deployed them in the trench on the spur to the northwest, roughly opposite from the redoubt with companies A and I of the 4th Minnesota across the cut. When Rowett arrived at the redoubt, he perceived the buildup to the west as the greatest threat. He had Colonel Perrin of the 7th Illinois order his three companies to the south to disengage and immediately rejoin the regiment. Captain Smith and his Company E took up a position in reserve near the house serving as the 93rd Illinois' headquarters. The other two rejoined the regiment in the redoubt.[126]

General French looked at his watch. It was almost 10:00 a.m., and there was still no large volume of musketry from the north indicating that Sears had started his attack. Knowing that time was critical, he sent orders to his brigadiers to advance. By the time the Rebels moved forward, it was 10:20 a.m.[127]

The opposing skirmish lines made contact first. It wasn't much of a fight. The skirmishers from the 93rd Illinois and 39th Iowa fired a few rounds and then immediately retreated in the face of the gray tide. The Confederates were right behind them. The Iowans were "driven back on a tangent," according to one survivor, and fell back on their three reserve companies, where the five continued to fire into the advancing butternuts. Lieutenant Ludlow was with the Illinoisans reconnoitering the ground when the attack started, and he fled with them. As they hopped over an old trench, the soldier next to him stooped over and grabbed a brick. The man threw it straight as a bullet and caught a Missourian behind them square in the face. The Rebel, chasing them at full speed, fell to the ground like a dead log, and the two continued their retreat as fast as their legs would carry them. The Illinoisans of the 93rd leapt over the redoubt and kept going, re-forming with Major Fisher below the Star Fort.[128]

The Missourians' main line came up to the rifle pits and halted. Once there, they re-formed and dressed their ranks. After a short rest, the advance resumed. With their skirmishers out of the way, the 39th and 7th opened fire. So did the crew of the Napoleon. Harvey M. Trimble of the 93rd Illinois described the onslaught:

Solid shot and shells, grape and canister from double-shotted cannon, and a hailstorm of bullets were rapidly and accurately poured into the ranks

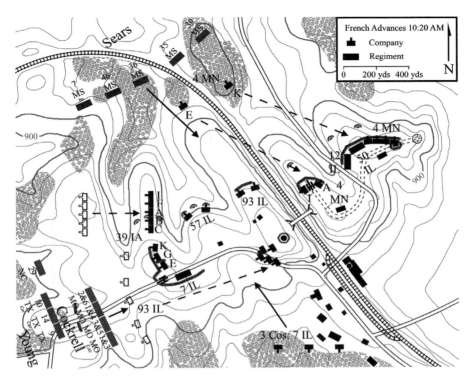

French's initial advance at approximately 10:30 a.m. The skirmishers of the 39th Iowa and 93rd Illinois are pushed back. *Courtesy of the author.*

> *of the Confederates as they recklessly advanced. They had been made*
> *to believe that they were to have an easy and speedy victory…And yet,*
> *notwithstanding their fearful losses at every step, they still advanced, faster*
> *and faster, until their whole force, west of the railroad cut, burst into an*
> *impetuous charge. The spectacle was sublime.*

The fire from the Napoleon caused considerable problems for the Rebels. "Grape and canister from that gun, double shotted, and a most galling fire of musketry, well directed and rapidly delivered, somewhat confused their lines and temporarily checked the advance of the enemy."[129]

The Missourians were hindered by the terrain as much as the shower of lead raining down on them. The ridge was so narrow that the outlying regiments had to struggle through three hundred yards of downed brush and trees. After fighting its way through this jungle, the left wing of the brigade descended into the ravine in front of the 39th Iowa and then up the opposing slope. The right likewise swung around and up to confront the 7th Illinois. Both wings halted at the abatis. This fatal pause gave the Federals even more time to rake the line with deadly fire. Captain Boyce of the 1st and 4th Missouri described the adrenaline-fueled scene: "Our first trouble was in scrambling through and over the abatis, which was, I think, thickly laced with telegraph wire, where we lost many men."

The Confederate line was in shambles. "When we reached the abatis," wrote Lieutenant Warren of the 3rd and 5th, "our advance was momentarily checked. By the time our line had made its way through the network of fallen timber all organization was gone. Companies and regiments were thoroughly mixed up." Exhausted, the Missourians halted about twenty yards from the earthworks and threw themselves to the ground. From there, they traded volleys with the Federals above them. More help was on the way for the defenders. Soon after the fighting started, the five companies of the 93rd Illinois under Major Fisher arrived to help stem the tide. They jumped into the trenches and added their rifles to the din.[130]

To the north, Sears' Brigade finally gained a position above the pass. On the left, the 35th and 39th Mississippi aligned to the east of the railroad tracks. The 7th, 46th and 36th spread out to the west. As the firing intensified at the redoubt, the brigade stepped off. Private J.V. Reddock in William Cambers's Company B was killed near the railroad. It, too, had to contend with several hundred yards of underbrush and felled trees. As Cockrell and Young approached Rowett from the west, Sears was poised to fall on their right and rear from the north.[131]

The fighting continued unabated in front of Rowett. The two sides traded shots at each other from close range—the Federals behind their earthworks and the Missourians only twenty yards away behind whatever cover they could find. Several hundred yards behind them, the men of Ector's Brigade halted at the first line of rifle pits. There, General Young addressed them. With a short inspirational speech, he told the men what was expected of them and where they were to charge the enemy's works. With a yell, they surged forward. Over and through the trees and obstacles they struggled. Rowett's men saw them coming and directed their fire into the approaching onslaught. Men fell with every step.[132]

Where was the 29th North Carolina to the left of the Texans? According to Major Ezekiel H. Hampton, commanding the 29th, it had to advance farther through the forest than the rest of the brigade, and when the men finally got into the open, they found themselves separated from the others.

Taking heavy fire, he ordered them to charge. Down into the ravine and back up they rushed, until within forty feet of the redoubt. They, along with the rest of the brigade, reached the prone Missourians, and the two lines merged. Hampton ordered his North Carolinians to the ground, where they rested and reloaded. After about five minutes, he ordered them to charge. Independently, officers along the line did likewise. The two brigades, hopelessly intermingled, leapt to their feet and scrambled over the parapet in front of them.[133]

What followed was one of the longest and most vicious hand-to-hand struggles of the war. "As our boys swarmed over the parapet," wrote Captain Boyce, "the bayonet was freely used by both sides, officers firing their pistols, and many throwing sticks and stones." Another Missourian agreed: "Here sabers clashed, bayonets crossed, and clubs and rocks hurled back and forth in the desperate struggle." Sergeant C.E. Dale of the 9th Texas was one of the first to mount the works, and he was shot dead. Sergeant John Rich, carrying the colors of the 29th North Carolina, cried, "Come ahead, boys!" and bound forward. He was almost immediately wounded and fell. The flag had barely touched the ground when Lieutenant E.B. Alexander, leading Company C, scooped it up. With Alexander yelling, "Come on, my brave boys!" the flag caught the breeze as he ran toward the Yankees. They shot him dead before he went fifteen feet. Sergeant W.J. Parker then took up the colors, sprinted the last few steps to the breastwork and planted the flag on the parapet. There a Federal shot him in the face. In the ensuing mêlée, Parker captured a horse, retrieved the flag and helped carry a wounded officer from his own company to safety.[134]

The Illinoisans and Iowans were giving as good as they got. William G. Powers of the 39th Iowa saw two men going at it across the head log. One particular Confederate was very close to the works, and as a fellow Iowan raised up to shoot, the Rebel fired at him. The round missed, and the Confederate, in desperation, grabbed a rock and hurled it at his opponent. He missed again, and the Iowan placed his rifle against the man's body and fired, deciding the contest.[135]

Like the North Carolinians at the end of the line, fighting swirled around the regimental flags of both sides. Major Owen A. Waddell, leading the 3rd and 5th Missouri, was shot on the parapet while waving the regiment's flag. Harry DeJarnette, carrying the flag of the 2nd and 6th Missouri, was shot down as he approached the works. The flag was immediately picked up and planted on the trench. Lieutenant Gillespie of the regiment broke his sword while trying to cut a Union soldier. The man survived but surrendered to the

The Confederates storm Rowett's Redoubt. *From Samuel G. French's* Two Wars.

The ravine in front of Rowett's Redoubt from the Cartersville Road. The Confederates advanced from left to right up the slope. *Photo by author.*

lieutenant. To their right, Captain Boyce of the 1st and 4th Missouri climbed to the top of the trench and came face to face with the regimental colors of the 93rd Illinois:

> As we gained the smoking, roaring parapet I observed the federal flag right in front and made for it; then the thought came up, "I have just gained my captain's commission, give others a chance," and I yelled at Sergt. John Ragland of our regiment, "John, go for those colors," and with a daring leap John tore them from their bearer's grasp, who received a clod of hard clay from the hand of the writer between the eyes at the same instant. The flag belonged to an Illinois regiment. John Ragland was sent to Richmond with this flag, and won his lieutenant's commission.[136]

Somewhere in the thick of the fray, Third Sergeant Randel M. Hartzell of the 39th Iowa was fighting while cradling the regiment's national flag. A Rebel jumped onto the parapet in front of him, grabbed the flag and demanded to have it. Hartzell indeed "let him have it," shooting the man dead. Immediately, Lieutenant M.W. Armstrong of the 10th Texas grabbed for it. Hartzell tried to gore him with his bayonet, but the officer was saved when a fellow Rebel clubbed the Iowan, knocking Hartzell down. The lieutenant came away with the colors and Hartzell as his prisoner.[137]

From his vantage point behind the lines, Captain Smith saw the Confederates overwhelm the 39th Iowa and capture its flag. Standing before his men, he shouted, "Boys, if we are ever going to do anything for our country, now is the time!" With that, he led his men forward. The fifty-two men in Company E made it the largest in the regiment. The company sprinted ahead, and when it arrived at the earthworks, it brought its Henry rifles into action. Their firepower momentarily pushed the Rebels back and stabilized the line. Captain Smith joined in and fired his own silver-plated Henry. One of his men later remarked that the language he used "was not appropriate for a Sunday school talk."[138]

Lieutenant Colonel James Redfield was doing his best to inspire the Iowans under his charge. He was just behind William Powers to the right of the road when he was shot in the arm. He continued exhorting his men to stand by the colors to the last, only to have another round shatter his leg. Falling, he managed to pull himself upright when a bullet finally pierced his heart. Other officers fell inspiring their men. Lieutenant Ayers, who had delivered Corse's reply, was killed fighting for the redoubt at about the same time as Redfield. Major Carter, who had instructed his Missourians to give no quarter, also perished in the charge. General Young was shot in the foot but continued to lead his men throughout the battle.[139]

The stubborn defense of the redoubt was sublime horror. One Missourian described it as the "only bayonet fight we were in during the war—God grant that we may never witness another scene like that." Captain Boyce later said, "This was, for the time engaged, the bloodiest fight we were ever in, and our loss was heavy. Corse's men fought like devils." Indeed. The defenders refused to give up. The only way to dislodge one of them was to knock him down and pull him out of his place.[140]

The pressure was greatest where the Cartersville Road bisected the works. Captain Smith and his Company E fought in and near the road. While the Henry rifles could throw a tremendous amount of lead downrange, not all of them worked flawlessly. Smith wrote years later:

> *I had a boy in my company named William H. Burwell. He was a very large man, not very tall, and on the left of the company. We would wait until we heard the rebels yell as they came up to the side of the ridge. They always yelled first and then fired. When we were reloading after one of these volleys, Burwell turned to me and said, "Captain, my gun is out of order." He couldn't get the cartridge into the chamber. Meantime I had loaded and emptied my gun several times. I said, "All right Billie. You take my gun and I will see if I can do anything with yours." I got down on my knees and got out one of those Barlow knives which you all remember, but I was unable to remove the difficulty.*[141]

The Mississippians broke the deadlock. Coming from the north, they filtered up the ravines and draws to the right. First they outflanked and poured a deadly enfilade fire into the five companies of the 39th Iowa outside the redoubt, forcing them to retreat. Once they did, the Mississippians began firing into the flank of the redoubt. At the Star Fort, General Corse saw them coming, but there wasn't much he could do about it. The general ran to the two companies on the north spur and encouraged them to hold on, but it was no use. The Mississippians swept over them, and they and Corse had to beat a hasty retreat to the main fort. Once inside, Corse realized that he desperately needed reinforcements if he was going to hold the pass west of the cut. He ordered Captain Flint to reach Tourtellotte, bring the 50th Illinois over to the west side of the tracks and reinforce Rowett. Unaware of the footbridge over the cut, Flint ran down the south side of the hill, crossed the tracks and ran back up the other side.

Once there, he gave Tourtellotte the orders, but it was too late. After forcing the Iowans to retreat, Sears's men slammed into the fight at the redoubt. It was too much for the defenders. After almost thirty minutes of ferocious face-to-face combat, those who could turned and fled. Some, like Colonel Perrin, ordered his 7th Illinois to withdraw, but others left on their own to avoid capture. Many indeed surrendered, but just as many turned and fought as they retired. Colonel Rowett was wounded and managed to make his way to safety, but his determined stand would leave his name forever bound to the fortification that his men struggled so hard to defend: Rowett's Redoubt. For all those racing for safety, the Star Fort became the beacon of their salvation, and all ran for its protection.[142]

Private Powers didn't leave the redoubt until the enemy had crossed the parapet and captured some of his company to his left. He was one of the lucky ones. His brother, Isaac, also in Company G, was killed defending the trench to the last. Powers turned and ran toward the Star Fort, passing on the way between a little shanty and an outdoor oven. He paused at an outhouse near the head of the ravine to the northwest of the Star Fort. There he turned and shot at his pursuers, reloading quickly. Picking up a discarded Henry rifle nearby, he sprinted for the Star Fort. When within a few steps of an artillery embrasure, a Rebel Minié ball struck him in the left forearm about an inch above his wrist. He dropped the Henry but made it into the fort without further harm.[143]

The mass of Confederates pursued. It was not an organized pursuit—more of a follow-up to the successful capture of the redoubt. Units were intermingled, and there was little organization at this point. Colonel John L. Camp of the 14th Texas fell wounded after taking only a few steps past the redoubt. Officers and NCOs attempted to restore order, shouting orders and getting their men into some sort of formation as quickly as possible. Two or three regiments began re-forming in the shelter of the Cartersville Road where it cut into the hillside. One of the three-inch rifles was packed with a double load of canister, a tin can filled with lead balls that exploded after leaving the muzzle of the cannon, effectively turning the weapon into a giant shotgun. Aiming at the forming column, the commander gave the order to fire. The gunner, James E. Croft, although wounded himself, had the lanyard taut and was in the act of pulling it. Suddenly, Major Fisher and the remnants of the 93rd, among others, surged up the hill and blocked the line of fire. An officer of the 93rd just managed to stay Croft's hand before he discharged the piece, preventing a swath of destruction cutting through their own men.

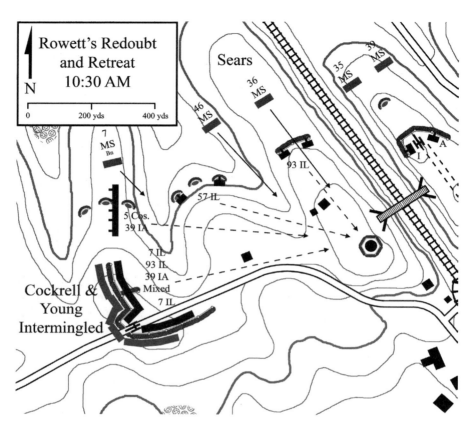

The fight at Rowett's Redoubt. The advance of Sears' Brigade forced everyone west of the railroad cut to fall back into the Star Fort. *Courtesy of the author.*

Union men began pouring into the ditch below the fort, clawing up the parapet and climbing through the cannon's embrasure. Those inside reached out and pulled the fleeing soldiers over the obstacles as best they could. With the Confederates gathering below, the cries for the cannon to fire reached a fever pitch, loud enough to be heard over the gunfire. Eventually, somebody remembered the sally port, or entrance, on the other side. Soon the cotton bales that blocked the exit were removed, and refugees scrambled into the fort. Among them was the Napoleon—its crew and nearby infantry had managed to drag it from the redoubt and save it from capture. With its front cleared, Croft pulled the lanyard, and the three-inch rifle roared to life. The balls of canister struck the ground just in front of the Rebels and ricocheted upward and forward, cutting a grisly swath through the formation. Bloodied,

The interior of the Star Fort looking northeast. The railroad gorge is on the other side of the far parapet. *Photo by author.*

the rest of the Confederates cleared the road and scrambled for cover in the nearby ravine or below the hill. Croft would later win the Medal of Honor for his actions.[144]

After forcing the Federal skirmishers to retreat, William Chambers and the 46th Mississippi had continued south. The enemy fire was heavy, but they finally struggled through the obstacles and abatis. Moving up the ravine northwest of the Star Fort, they made their way to a small shelf on the edge of the slope that offered some protection from the incoming fire. Over the lip of the shelf was a flat area on which lay some of the tents of the garrison; the Star Fort loomed beyond. The Mississippi regiments were hopelessly intermingled. The officers did the best they could to re-form, and then someone called out, "Forward!" Somebody else bellowed, "The 46th goes forward!" and the line surged ahead. Chambers, caught up in the moment, crested the rise, waved his hat above his head and shouted, "C'mon boys! The 46th goes ahead!" With a wild yell, about thirty of them dashed through the tents toward the fort. A hailstorm of lead greeted them. When within a few yards of the fort, Colonel Clark, commanding the 46th, took the regimental colors and waved them aloft to encourage his men. He was soon shot down. In less than thirty seconds, only Chambers and Lieutenant R.B. Henderson were left standing. A ball struck Chambers's rifle, flattened the barrel and shattered the stock. Suddenly, Henderson staggered over to Chambers, crying out, "Brother Chambers, I am gone!"[145]

Exposed in the open, he caught Henderson and eased him to the ground. "My dear brother," said Chambers, "what is the ground of your hope?"

"My only hope is Christ," said the wounded man. "Pray for me." The two began praying together. Henderson grasped his hand, and his body jerked. Chambers felt his clothing and equipment move and a sharp, stinging pain in his shoulder as another round struck him at the same time. "Oh brother, I have received my third wound!" cried Henderson "Good bye!" There was a spasm in his hand, and suddenly the grasp went limp. Looking down, Chambers saw that Henderson had been shot in the head. Finding that he could no longer use his arm, he lay down behind the body of his friend.[146]

The Confederates had been stopped short of the Star Fort, but it was a temporary reprieve. The struggle for the fort was rapidly becoming the focus of the entire battle.

Chapter 11

Trusting in the God of Battles

As soon as Corse assigned responsibility for the east side of the tracks to Tourtellotte, the colonel rode over to take charge of his command. What he found must have been encouraging. The 4th Minnesota, his largest regiment, had two companies in the Eastern Redoubt—Company B faced north and Company G south. Companies A and I held the northern redoubt next to the railroad tracks above the cut, with A on the right and I on the left. One of the 12th Wisconsin Battery's three-inch rifles had been wheeled into position there to bolster its defenses. Companies E and K were still out in front on the skirmish line, and the remaining four companies held the trench along the crest. The 12th and 50th Illinois were also in the earthworks on the crest. To the south, seven companies of the 18th Wisconsin were still guarding the approaches from that direction. In all, Tourtellotte had about 1,058 infantry at his disposal. Finally, the remaining three-inch rifle and the Napoleon from the 12th Wisconsin were in the Eastern Redoubt.[147]

Scores of Minnesotans were in an awkward position. They had enlisted on September 26, 1861, and signed up for three years. Their enlistments had expired nine days earlier. Yet they were being kept in the service. The reason, at least as expressed by the men, was that they were being denied their discharges in order to swell the ranks of the regiment with the new recruits. More men in the ranks authorized more officers to lead them, and those officers now serving could expect promotions. It is doubtful that the men appreciated being exposed to the possibility of death after their entitled discharge for the sake of a new bar or eagle on the shoulder of one of their ambitious leaders.[148]

A large number of the Minnesotans were also raw recruits. They had only been issued rifles a few days before. The previous night, as they were waiting for reinforcements to arrive, the seasoned veterans of the 4th had trained the new soldiers in the dark. They practiced and drilled the procedure for firing and loading—on-the-job training at its finest, born of necessity. Others in the regiment finalized other preparations. For example, several of the men from various companies had placed markers on the ground at intervals from one hundred to five hundred yards from the fort. These markers were intended to gauge the distance to any approaching enemy and assist the men with their aim. In addition, for easy access, a stockpile of ammunition was collected and stored near the eastern end of the footbridge over the cut.[149]

It didn't take long after Tourtellotte's return for the action to heat up in the west. The men in the trenches heard the fighting near Rowett's Redoubt increase in intensity and volume. Closer, the butternuts in Sears' Brigade pushed steadily south. When the pressure became too great, Companies E and K sprinted back to their main line and took their place in the earthworks. Company E redeployed just below the headquarters building facing south, overlooking the storehouse below and keeping a sharp eye to its safety. Tourtellotte made a few final adjustments to his line. First, he had Colonel Hanna send Koehler's 12th Illinois across the Tennessee Road and assist Companies A and I. It quickly ran and took position on the left of Company I, facing due west across the cut. It were exposed, with no earthworks to protect it. The 50th Illinois soon followed. However, it stopped at the saddle between the Eastern Redoubt and the hill above the tracks. It faced north, with its right on the road, where it could cover the draw in front of it.[150] •

William Chambers lay in front of the Star Fort across the tracks, still behind the body of his dead friend. He could feel and hear rifle balls as they struck the corpse. As he watched, the 12th Illinois lined up on the hillside across the tracks and fired into the flank of the Mississippians. He observed a Union officer "jump up and wave his sword in exultation over the result of the volley." Frustrated and helpless, Chambers longed for a rifle so that he could shoot the man down. Looking back up at the Star Fort, he could see the color of the eyes of the men as they raised up to fire. Realizing how helpless he was, he resolved to get out as soon as he could. He considered taking a few things with him. A bar of soap rested atop a nearby stump. Several "magazine rifles," probably Henrys, lay nearby. Ultimately, he decided against it. During a lull, he struggled to his feet, ran past the tents and made

The trenches on the northern slope of the hill occupied by the 4th Minnesota. The Eastern Redoubt is to the upper right. *Photo by author.*

it below the small crest of the hill with no further injuries. However, it was a near thing. After fainting and reviving shortly thereafter, he found that a new Minié ball had struck his cartridge box and imbedded itself in the leather. Half of it was protruding on the side facing his body.[151]

The 50th Illinois and the rest of 4th Minnesota didn't have to wait long for the attack to their front. The 35th and 39th Mississippi swept forward in conjunction with the assault to the west. Unfortunately, they were hopelessly outnumbered. While French may has gained numerical superiority at Rowett's Redoubt, it was at the expense of the attack in the east. The two Mississippi regiments, at a best guess, probably only had about two hundred to three hundred men. At worst, they were outnumbered three to one, and the men above them were strongly entrenched with artillery support. The outcome was never really in doubt.

The rest of Sears' Brigade found little success to the west. The 36th and 46th Mississippi, after overrunning the outpost south of the Star Fort and putting Corse to his heels, were stopped cold by the fire from Company I and the 12th Illinois. Their fire from across the tracks struck the Mississippians square in the flank as they tried to advance on the Star Fort and put them to ground far short of their objective. Likewise, the 35th and 39th Mississippi to the east of the tracks quickly took cover in the face of the storm of lead and iron hurled their way.[152]

Still, it wasn't entirely a one-way fight. The struggle for the northern redoubt was particularly intense, since the men there were essentially fighting in three directions. Company I in the northern redoubt didn't occupy trenches as deep as those sheltering Company A to its right. It alternately fought and dug into the earth, using anything handy including poles from its nearby tents and wood from ammunition or ration boxes. It ultimately suffered three killed and seven wounded, two of whom later died. The 12th Illinois to its left was completely exposed, losing one officer and five men to wounds in that position. The gunners manning the three-inch rifle suffered severely. They had no cover whatsoever and were reduced to lying flat on their backs, passing ammunition between themselves and only reaching up to load their cannon. In the end, all were either killed or wounded.[153]

Stories of bravery were common. Ephram Dudley, fighting with Company A, was mortally wounded. As he lay dying, he said, "I would not care about dying, if I had fought all day; but I regret being killed after having fired but three shots." John Young and George Rogers of the same company were among those fighting with expired enlistments and should have been on their way north. Instead, they died fighting behind a barricade of wood and red clay far from home. Lieutenant George M.D. Lambert in Company A used two rifles, as did many others. When one got too hot, he would switch to the other. Alternatively, some would load rifles and pass them forward to another, who would do the shooting. Sergeants Oscar O. Jaquith and Philip W. Fix used two rifles continually in this manner, having them loaded by recruits who did not have the training yet to use them effectively. Both of their shoulders were badly bruised by the end of the fight. The next day, they were unavailable for duty because of their injuries.[154]

Private Isaac Russell began the day in the hospital recovering from typhoid fever. Unfortunately, a cannon ball crashed through the building, after which Russell thought better of his chances on the front line. He returned to Company A and asked for his gear. He fought the rest of the day even though he could barely stand. The recoil of his rifle knocked him down with each discharge. Yet he got up, reloaded and fired again each time. Sylvanus Allen, a Methodist minister in the company, had previously set up a wooden booth across the ravine from their position from which to preach. It became a favorite

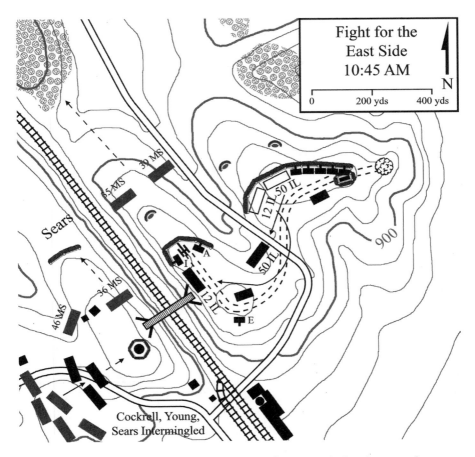

The fight east of the railroad tracks. The 12th and 50th Illinois redeployed to meet the oncoming Confederates. *Courtesy of the author.*

shelter for some of the Mississippians, and Allen devoted his attention, and his rifle, to those who would use his "gospel shop" in that manner. After the battle, he reportedly found eight dead Rebels in it. In all, Company A alone fired 9,400 rounds during the day, an average of 293 per man.[155]

To the east, the 50th Illinois and the remainder of the 4th Minnesota fought equally hard. The Mississippians emerged from the wood line to the north and fired a volley. Corporal Henry Ritchy of the 50th was struck in the forehead and killed instantly. Lewis R. Collins was standing next to him and believed that Ritchy was the first of the 50th to fall that day. The Rebels got to within one hundred yards before the command rang out to fire. According to Collins, "At first they wavered, then stopped and finally retreated back, pell-mell, into the timber." Lieutenant Colonel William Hanna of the 50th reported three separate Confederate charges against his line, resulting in heavy losses. His men were also fighting exposed, with no earthworks. The 4th Minnesota to their right had a better time of it, as it was well protected.

Throughout the battle, Colonel Tourtellotte went along the lines encouraging his men. He relayed to them that Sherman was at Kennesaw and that help was on the way. Such encouragement probably inspired the men to fight harder, though none as hard as Almon H. Cottrell. He was wounded early in the battle and had his arm amputated in the field. Instead of lying down and resting, however, he got back up and carried ammunition to the men along the lines. The exertion ultimately cost him; he died of lockjaw, or tetanus, a few days after the battle. One of the lucky ones was Reverend Charles H. Savidge of Company H. A ball struck his chest, but a testament in his pocket absorbed the impact and stopped any further penetration.[156]

When Captain Flint arrived with Corse's request for reinforcements Tourtellotte responded immediately. Tourtellotte interpreted Corse's order to mean that only one regiment was needed on the west side. He ordered Colonel Hanna to send one of his two regiments across. However, Hanna apparently misunderstood. He later reported that he "received orders to report with my command on the west side of the railroad at the fort" and took "my command," including both the 12th and 50th Illinois. The two regiments moved rapidly to the west. The 12th, already in line facing west, simply moved by the left flank down the hill and crossed the tracks. It did not do so unscathed. Myrick's artillery to the south opened up a "heavy and severe fire" on the exposed bluecoats that "killed and wounded some," according to Captain Koehler. Upon arriving at the Star Fort, the captain found the fort, ditch and surrounding rifle pits brimming with men. Amid the chaos, he stationed the 12th outside the fort facing south, covering the village itself.[157]

Hanna and his men were not far behind or, more likely, arrived at about the same time. They disengaged from the fight to the north and ran at the double-quick down the hill to the tracks. The artillery barrage that fell on Koehler's men also deluged Hanna's, as did Confederates who had advanced into the village itself. The mass of charging Illinoisans scattered the few Rebels among the buildings. With a bit of hyperbole, Hanna wrote of this charge in his report, "Bravely and nobly did the officers and men of the Fiftieth Illinois Infantry maintain their order, marching up with that determined feeling which only visits the brave soldier, to conquer or

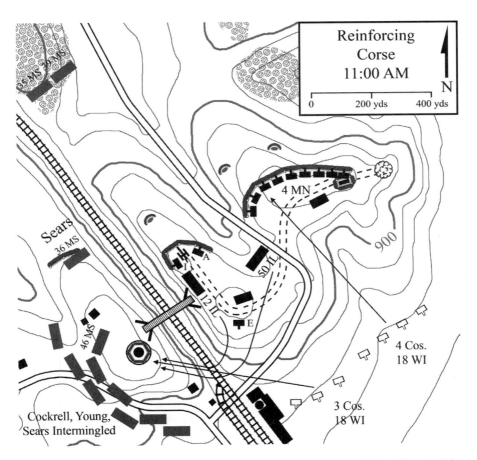

The 12th Illinois, 50th Illinois and half of the 18th Wisconsin moved to reinforce Corse inside the Star Fort. *Courtesy of the author.*

die, trusting in the God of battles for that glorious result which followed victory." When the Illinoisans arrived at the western summit, they found that one of their flagstaffs had been shot off three different times during the run. Most of the men quickly formed outside the fort facing south, with their left on the cut just above the tracks. They were probably next to, or near, the 12th, but accounts from the participants are vague and unclear. Colonel Hanna, in his report, could have been referring the position of both the 12th and 50th, as most of the men in both were outside the fort facing south. However, some of the 50th did continue on into the Star Fort and fought from there.[158]

Captain Flint was with them. He had preceded the 50th on its journey. When he reported to Corse in the Star Fort, Flint was informed, with considerable amusement, that he had run up the hill with both hands covering his bottom amid the deluge of shells from the south. For Flint it was an act "of which...I was entirely unconscious."[159]

With the Confederate artillery and its infantry support to the south, and the brigades of Cockrell and Ector approaching the village from the west, the 18th Wisconsin was in a perilous location. It was in danger of being cut off. Realizing this, Lieutenant Colonel Jackson ordered the regiment to retreat as the fight at Rowett's Redoubt reached its apogee. On the way back, the regiment split. Four companies fell back with Jackson to the Eastern Redoubt, and three companies went west to the Star Fort. The Rebels were not far behind. Colonel Julius A. Andrews, commanding the infantry supporting the batteries, sent Colonel David Coleman with forty men of his 39th North Carolina northward in pursuit. The Tarheels "advanced rapidly, cheering and firing briskly," but probably followed, rather than pushed, the 18th Wisconsin as it retired. Coleman and his men took shelter along the railroad embankment and surrounding terrain just south of the village and kept up a constant fire on the Federals above.[160]

The battle for the pass was reaching its climax. One more determined assault by French's men could overrun the Star Fort and likely force the surrender of the garrison. However, it would not be easy. Except for the 4th Minnesota and part of the 18th Wisconsin, all of the remaining Union infantry were crammed into the Star Fort, its ditch and the nearby surrounding rifle pits.

Chapter 12

We Hold Out

W hile French and Corse were struggling for control of Allatoona, events elsewhere would have a profound effect on the outcome of the battle and the history written afterward. To the north, railroad engineers and Union officers were struggling to bring reinforcements to the beleaguered garrison. The locomotive that had dropped off Corse and his men at the pass had immediately reversed and raced back to Rome. Waiting there was the rest of his Fourth Division, eager to board the train and hurry to the aid of their comrades. Unfortunately, the line broke again seven miles east of Rome. The train arrived at the break at 7:30 a.m. However, before the break, a smaller train had been assembled at Rome, consisting of three boxcars, two platform cars and two cabooses. This small assembly shuttled portions of the 7th Iowa and 52nd Illinois from the division's First Brigade and the remaining companies of the 57th Illinois down to the break. They boarded the train on the east side and, under the command of the 57th's Lieutenant Colonel Frederick J. Hurlbut, "moved with all possible dispatch to Cartersville." Back at Rome, other regiments of the division were shuttled to the break as fast as they could be loaded and moved.[161]

General Raum was also on his way to Allatoona from Cartersville. As the battle was raging, he led a small contingent south, including General McCook, Captain Zickerick, two or three staff and half a dozen orderlies. They arrived near the battlefield but remained hidden from view by a "heavy skirt of timber." While observing the fight, one of French's staff officers, traveling on foot and likely relaying messages to and from General Sears, came too close to the party. Faced with a dozen armed men on horseback, the hapless staffer was forced to surrender. They waited a short time for the rest of the Rowett's brigade to arrive and then turned around and rode back to Cartersville.[162]

Back at Smyrna Camp Ground, Sherman issued his orders for October 5 to his various commands. While he was concerned for the garrison at Allatoona, his actions showed that he also was operating with a defensive mindset until his armies were concentrated. His orders kept his infantry in a loose arc around Marietta. He directed Stanley's Army of the Cumberland, which began the day with the Fourth Corps in the works on Little Kennesaw, and the Fourteenth at Nickajack Creek to control the Sandtown Road to Allatoona. To achieve this, the army was to march to and occupy Pine Mountain to the northwest. To the south, he ordered Howard's Army of the Tennessee to move west and cover the Marietta Road at Kolb's Farm. With Howard on the left and Stanley in the center, he ordered Cox's Army of the Ohio to extend the line to the right. With one of his aides, he sent a note to Cox directing him exactly where to take up his position: "I have sent Colonel Warner to you to explain your position, which is to the front and right of Kenesaw, following the Big Shanty road about a mile, and from the base of the mountain to a fortified ridge, from which you overlook cleared ground very extensive. Leave your train near the base of the mountain." Even Cox, in his journal written that day, stated that he only advanced one mile beyond Kennesaw Mountain by the end of the day, mostly because Howard's wagons clogged the road to Marietta, slowing his progress.[163]

In his report written the following January, Sherman said that he ordered Cox to "move rapidly from the base of Kennesaw, due west, aiming to reach the road from Allatoona to Dallas, threatening the rear of the forces attacking Allatoona." Decades later in his memoirs, Sherman would write, "I ordered the Twenty-third Corps (General Cox) to march due west on the Burnt Hickory road, and to burn houses or piles of brush as it progressed, to indicate the head of column, hoping to interpose this corps between Hood's main army at Dallas and the detachment then assailing Allatoona. The rest of the army was directed straight for Allatoona, northwest, distant eighteen miles." Unfortunately, neither was true, or at the very least, no contemporary order exists to corroborate it. In fact, his orders delivered by Colonel Warner appear to contradict them. Either Sherman's memory on the subject was faulty, or he had begun to embellish the facts even by January 1865 to make it look like he did more to support the besieged Allatoona garrison than he actually did.[164]

The only unit Sherman did order to Allatoona on the fifth was Garrard's Second Division. The cavalry began the day located north of Kennesaw Mountain, skirmishing with Armstrong's horsemen where they had previously covered Stewart's Corps destroying the railroad. Sherman ordered it to cover Stanley's move to Pine Mountain. The division marched to the vicinity of Hardshell Church, also referred to as Golgatha or Gilgal Church. In an order with no time stamp, he directed General Elliott to have Kilpatrick move south and screen Howard and have Garrard move to Allatoona the evening of the fifth:

> *Order Kilpatrick to Howards left, to report to Howard. Dispatch Garrard to-night to Allatoona, making a circuit to the right, and to learn if possible the state of affairs there. I think the place was assaulted to-day, but repulsed. The day was so hazy we could get but few messages.*

His guess that the place was assaulted but repulsed strongly indicates that the fighting had already abated when he issued the order to Elliott, probably in mid- to late afternoon. Regardless of what he wrote after the war, the fact is that he issued no orders to any of his units to rush to the aid of the garrison while the battle was still raging.[165]

General Elliott was helping Corse and his men, although perhaps inadvertently. During the day, one of his cavalry regiments, the 4th U.S. Regulars, rode toward Allatoona, passed Kemp's Mill and drove cavalry pickets from their camps. General Stanley, who observed them from atop Pine Mountain, estimated that they traveled about two miles past the mill. However, this was at about 3:00 p.m. They would have been much farther south during the time their presence would have had any bearing on the struggle to the north. These Confederates were probably from Armstrong's cavalry brigade, and their small encounter would add fuel to postwar recriminations.[166]

Hood, for his part, remained static around Lost Mountain. The army, however, was on marching orders, ready to move at a moment's notice. They were joined in the morning by Stewart, with Loring and Walthall's Divisions in tow, having returned from their foray against the railroad.[167]

The fifth may have dawned clear and bright for French at Allatoona, but for Lieutenant Fish atop Kennesaw, the day began in a white cocoon of impenetrable fog that he said "hung around the brow of Kenesaw like a funeral pall." He spent the morning in a hastily built hut used for shelter, with his eyeglass focused on Allatoona and Lost Mountain. The fog started to lift at about 8:00 a.m., and he began signaling Allatoona. For two and a half hours, his team attempted to

Interior view of the Eastern Redoubt looking east. The signal tree was a few dozen yards down the slope from the opposite parapet. *Photo by author.*

establish contact with the garrison. Among them was Sherman himself. After awakening at his headquarters at Smyrna Camp Ground and issuing the day's orders, he made his way north to Marietta and then continued to the summit of Kennesaw. The general was impatient for news and, according to Fish, "could not understand (or would not) that there was an obstruction in the way that eye of mortal man could not penetrate." Although offered the opportunity to use the eyeglass several times, Sherman refused.[168]

Finally, at 10:35 a.m., they saw a signal from Allatoona. As Fish was at the eyeglass reading the flag motions and writing down the corresponding numbers, a figure walked onto a rock in front of him, interfering with his field of view. After a few choice and impolite words, the man moved. As it turns out, the figure was none other than Sherman himself. Apparently, he did not take the admonition to heart, for he was soon in the hut with Fish and one of his assistants translating the coded message:

We hold out. General Corse here.

According to Sherman, "It was a source of great relief, for it gave me the first assurance that General Corse had received his orders, and that the place was adequately garrisoned." The signal station worked hard to see and decode additional messages from Allatoona, but none was forthcoming. Fish and the other signal stations became swamped for the remainder of the morning and early afternoon observing the Confederates around Lost Mountain and signaling orders to the armies assembling around Kennesaw and Pine Mountain.[169]

At Allatoona, the signal station was trying just as hard to communicate with Kennesaw. Lieutenant Adams and his men tried to signal from outside the fort early in the morning, but with the Confederates so close, it became far too dangerous. They had to move into the Eastern Redoubt at about 10:00 a.m. There were twelve signalmen in the detachment, and as the Rebels approached the fortifications, Adams dismissed nine of them to take up their arms and help man the earthworks. Adams was apparently too ill to perform duties too strenuous and had Private James W. McKenzie manning the flag, assisted by Private Frank A. West.

When they finally established contact with Fish on Kennesaw, they began a short message under fire. According to Adams, McKenzie began the message, but West soon relieved him and finished it. West, however, had a different version of the events. He was not part of Adams's command. In fact, he was a signalman in the Army of the Cumberland and was on his way to rejoin that army in Atlanta. He was in Acworth on the third when the Confederate broke the railroad and had to retreat north to avoid capture. He attached himself to the garrison, and even Adams admitted that he wasn't aware of West's presence until he volunteered to help that morning. West, in an 1892 letter to the veterans of the 4th Minnesota, stated that McKenzie manned the telescope observing Kennesaw, while he stood on the embankment of the Eastern Redoubt and waved the six-foot flag. It took about four minutes, and during that brief period, several bullets passed through the flag, some struck the staff and others went through his clothing.[170]

General French was also receiving messages from outside his command. He received a note from Armstrong shortly before, or just immediately after, he sent forward Cockrell and Young. It was marked 7:00 a.m. It was a short message and asked at what time French would move toward New Hope and pass Acworth. It also informed him that the Federals had moved up east of the railroad above Kennesaw and had encamped there last night. French had seen the Federals above Kennesaw from Acworth, and they would have been Garrard's cavalry. Cox's Army of the Ohio, the only other infantry to march north of Marietta during the day, would have still been south of that city at about 7:00 a.m., struggling to make its way through the traffic jam caused by Howard's wagon train. In fact, the Army of the Ohio didn't move through Marietta until three o'clock in the afternoon. Therefore, Cox's men couldn't have been the ones French observed the night before from Acworth. There could have been infantry from Vandever's small command present, and they were not very numerous, but Armstrong would not have known that. Still, the message couldn't have been too alarming, and French had to concentrate on another important mission: the final assault on the Star Fort.[171]

Chapter 13

Silence Sir! Or I Will Have You Shot!

The fight for the Star Fort continued unabated. In fact, there was not much of a lull. The first charge for the fort, the blasting of the assaulting Confederates with the three-inch rifle and Hanna's rush to reinforce the western end of the cut all occurred simultaneously. Cockrell and Ector's men rushed forward in a desperate attempt to overrun the stronghold. Some occupied the village on the east side of the tracks. Others rushed the fort. The defenders killed Lieutenant J.P. Bates of the 9th Texas just as he reached the ditch. Some of his fellow Texans charged with him. Others remained at Rowett's Redoubt to sharp-shoot at the Federals. Men of the 14th Texas charged through and up the ravine to the northwest of the Star Fort and occupied the house and outbuildings located to the north. Major Hampton maintained that his 29th North Carolina got within twenty-five yards of the fort before being forced to seek cover. They remained there the rest of the battle firing at the defenders. Henry Pool of the 10th Texas was shot between the eyes during the assault.[172]

According to Henry Trimble of the 93rd Illinois, the Confederates launched four separate assaults against the Star Fort in the hour between 11:00 a.m. and noon. The defenders were formed several ranks deep. Three men often worked together. One man stood at the parapet and fired the rifles, while the other two loaded. That way, the shooter could merely hand his spent rifle back and receive a charged one immediately. As the battle wore on, large numbers of the Springfield rifles burst because of the built-up powder and lead in the barrels. The cotton bales at the sally port caught fire, adding to the smoke and choking atmosphere. Soon the wounded began to pile up. Lieutenant Colonel Hanna was wounded and knocked out of action shortly after entering the fort. Lewis Collins of the 50th was shot seven times, but only one drew blood—a round clipped his ear. One round went through two feet of dirt and struck him squarely in the temple as he was reloading. He tumbled over and was incoherent for about five minutes. Then, he slowly put his hand to his head, expecting a mortal wound, but thankfully found no sign of blood or serious injury.[173]

Sears continued his attack from the north. Unfortunately, the fire from Companies A and I across the tracks stymied any attempt to attack the Star Fort from the north. At 12:30 p.m., Sears sent a message to French:

> *Our men are fighting bravely. Will get up a grand charge as soon as the men rest a little. We will take this work, if possible. Men are greatly fatigued. We are in enemy's works, but have not the fort yet. The yells of your men do us great good.*

Unfortunately, Sears's new attack was no more successful than the previous ones. The 35th and 39th Mississippi attempted to use the ravine containing the Tennessee Road as a covered avenue of approach, but it was a trap. The fire from Company A above them to their right, and the rest of the Minnesotans to their left, brought their charge to a halt. Those who weren't killed or able to get away had to find shelter at the bottom of the draw. There was no way out.[174]

Major James Edson ordered the regiment's adjutant, Lieutenant Wilson W. Rich, to take a company out and fire into those trapped in the ravine. Rich found and took out Company H to the exposed hillside, where they fired volleys across the way. The exchange was not one-sided; the Confederates returned fire as well. Finding it "too hot," Rich ran back to the earthworks and found Lieutenant Colonel Jackson of the 18th Wisconsin. Rich asked him for an additional company to reinforce Company H, but Jackson declined. Coming upon Company C of the 4th, Rich informed its captain that he had no orders for a second company but that needed it. The captain cheerfully said yes, and off they went. Rich then returned to Colonel Jackson. He persuaded Jackson to come out to the two companies and look for himself, but the Colonel again declined to help, stating that he thought two companies was enough.[175]

Companies A and I, having fought hard all day in their redoubt, were nearing the end of their ammunition supply. Colonel Tourtellotte, who

Interior of the Star Fort looking northwest. The fiercest fighting and heaviest casualties occurred along this stretch of parapet. *Photo by author.*

was present at the moment, asked for someone to get more cartridges stacked near the headquarters house. Washington Muzzy, a member of the band, volunteered. He ran the hundred yards to the house, shouldered one of the hundred-pound boxes and returned with it. The entire run was along the crest of the spur, fully exposed to Confederate view. Just as he was about to reach the shelter of the redoubt, he tumbled and fell heavily. Assuming that he had been shot, another member of the band got up and retrieved the box. As it turned out, Muzzy had merely tripped in his haste and was uninjured, except perhaps to his pride. The ammunition was soon distributed among the Minnesotans and on its way to the Rebels in a slightly more lethal form.[176]

Colonel Tourtellotte continually rode the lines. Everybody's blood was up, and tensions were high. The colonel saw one man jump on top of the earthworks, shake his fist at the enemy and dare the enemy to come on. He was immediately shot down but luckily survived. Every man was engaged in defending the pass, and that included a few unusual combatants. Tourtellotte ordered his black servant to distribute ammunition, as he did not want to spare anybody who could be shooting. The man afterward found a rifle of his own and took his place on the firing lines. So did a few civilians, most likely railroad employees. Tourtellotte made them fire rifles to defend the pass or carry the wounded to the surgeons. Finally, at about 1:00 p.m., his luck ran out. He was shot halfway between the headquarters building and Companies A and I. Afterward, he sat on the spur where he could overlook the battle and sent orders via his servant, civilians or hospital attendants. Major Edson would later claim that the colonel sent him ten messages, almost all the same, basically stating, "If he allowed the enemy to cross that road [the Tennessee Road] running down the hill to the north I would never forgive him."[177]

The fighting at the Star Fort had turned into a stalemate. One Federal described it as "the Confederates still clinging to every hillside and every knoll and every ravine, and every house and outbuilding, and every other place that afforded the least protection from our fire, maintained the battle with wonderful pertinacity…they kept the air, over the forts and rifle pits, literally full of bullets all the time." Concealed behind stumps, logs and depressions in the ground, the Confederates fired at any man who dared raise himself over the parapet or who exposed himself in front of one of the artillery embrasures. Still, when a Rebel showed himself, they returned the favor as best they could. As an extra measure against a final, all-out assault, the unused Henry rifles of the 7th Illinois were stacked against the walls of the fort, ready for use at a moment's notice.[178]

Union flag bearers continued to suffer. Corporal Samuel Walker was carrying the colors of the 7th Illinois inside the Star Fort when a bullet struck the staff and snapped it in two. Before the flag touched the ground, Walker had grasped the shattered staff and mounted the parapet. There, as the future regimental historian would write with a bit of flourish, "he waved it until a minie went crashing through his brain—waved it until he fell, and there in blood under the grand old flag, the pride of his heart, the glory of his manhood, he died—died for the flag, died for his country, died for liberty." It was hyperbole well deserved and earned. The color sergeant of the 12th Illinois with the national colors was struck down, and W.H. Hallet picked the flag up. Hallet had already been shot three times. One struck his groin but was stopped by a coin in his pocket. Another struck his cap box, while the third bent his rifle and rendered it useless. He would survive the battle and carry the flag through the rest of the day and later on the March to the Sea.[179]

Remains of the small redoubt occupied by Companies A and I of the 4th Minnesota, as well as one three-inch ordnance rifle, looking east. *Photo by author.*

At about noon, General French received a message that changed everything. It was another message from Armstrong, written at 9:00 a.m.:

> *My scouts report enemy's infantry advancing up the railroad. They are now entering Big Shanty. They have a cavalry force east of the railroad.*

Alarming, to be sure. If true, it meant Union infantry was marching up the railroad and could, by the end of the day, come up behind French and trap him. They could also go west and cut off the direct road back to the rest of the army at Lost Mountain. Unfortunately, it wasn't true, at least from the standpoint of receiving accurate information on which to make an informed decision. The Army of the Cumberland was marching for Pine Mountain. Due to a bend in the railroad, it's possible that its line of march may have made it look like it was following the tracks north. This is the most likely explanation for infantry "advancing up the railroad." The Army of the Tennessee was south of Kennesaw at Kolb's Farm. The Army of the Ohio was south of Marietta. The only infantry near Marietta, much less east or north of the town, would have been Vandever's limited garrison. Composed of the small 41st, 32nd Illinois and those of the 14th and 15th Illinois battalion that hadn't been captured two days earlier, Vandever's infantry were hardly in a position to force their way north to Big Shanty, and nowhere is it written that they did so. If they were "advancing up the railroad," then Armstrong's scouts seriously overinflated normal skirmishing and scouting from them. Finally, the only Union cavalry "east of the railroad" would have been Garrard's division. However, it was headed west toward Gilgal Church, as previously ordered. The 4th U.S. Cavalry, north of Kemp's Mill, was nowhere near the railroad, Big Shanty or "east of the railroad." Although French would later cite its presence as the force that Armstrong was reporting, it simply could not have been. At the time, however, French could not have known any of this and had to take the message at face value. He would have to decide his next course of action, and he would have to do it soon.[180]

Inside the Star Fort, the strain was beginning to show. One man was heard to say, "It is no use, we cannot hold this fort." Unfortunately, he said it within earshot of General Corse, who thundered out for all to hear, "Silence sir! Or I will have you shot! We will hold this fort. Never let me hear such cowardly words from one of my men again." Even these types of threats weren't enough to stop men from losing their nerve. Some gave up fighting and sought shelter where they could. Many lay down at the foot of the parapet, "playing dead," as Lieutenant Ludlow put it. The wounded and those still fighting either ignored them, sat on them or stood on them as they raised themselves over the parapet to fire. However, others continued to hold up well, even rising to the occasion. The 50th Illinois' Second Assistant Surgeon Albert G. Pickett was wounded but continued to attend to the men around him. He also helped load rifles for others to fire. For his bravery, Colonel Hanna mentioned him in his official report, and decades later, he was cited in the regimental history. Another standout was a black man fighting tenaciously alongside the soldiers. He was not an enlisted man and could have been an officer's servant much like the one employed by Tourtellotte. According to one officer, "Time after time, it seemed to me a dozen—he would in a partially protected place, load his piece, and deliberately step in front of the opening in the parapet and deliver his fire with utmost coolness. His clothing was cut in several placed, but otherwise he escaped without injury."[181]

The Texans in the house to the northwest continued to plague the fort. Captain Flint noticed occasional puffs of smoke from holes in the chimney

Barnard photograph of the Star Fort interior looking out the sally port. The redoubt of the 4th Minnesota's Companies A and I are to the right. *National Archives, 533401.*

and suspected that it was being used as shelter for sharpshooters. It was about 1:00 p.m., and Flint brought it to Corse's attention. His commander, not a tall man to begin with, was looking over the parapet at the house on his tiptoes when Flint felt hot blood on his cheek. Thinking that he had been shot, he brought his right hand to his face just in time to use that arm to catch the falling general. Corse had been grazed by a shot that cut a furrow in his cheek and clipped his ear. It bled profusely and knocked Corse insensible for about thirty to forty minutes. Flint found Corse a sheltered place, where the general sat atop "one of those 'living corpses' who preferred to endure the pain and discomfort of his position rather than get up and face the deadly music that filled the air."[182]

The sharpshooters had to be dealt with. Inopportunely, the three-inch rifle facing that direction had jammed some time before. Replacing it proved to be a major undertaking. General Corse had ordered it to be moved and replaced by the remaining rifle, but he was wounded before the operation was completed. The major impediment was the carpet of dead and wounded that covered the interior of the fort. The floor was covered with prostrate men who could not move on their own. Macabre "roads" had to be made through the human debris. The dead could be moved with impunity, but the wounded required a delicate touch. As they worked, enemy balls continued their deadly work. Major Fisher of the 93rd Illinois was severely wounded in his left side as he passed one of the open embrasures, and command passed to Captain Clark Gray. In fact, the firing was so intense that the wooden gabions on either side of the embrasures were shot to pieces. With no means left to hold the dirt in place, the openings began to crumble. Eventually, however, the serviceable rifle was manhandled into place, and the chimney, if not parts of the house itself, was "knocked to flinders." Three exploding shells blasted the house and one into each of the outbuildings. Those Confederates not killed or wounded fled to the ravine for safety, chased by a hail of bullets from the fort.

The gunner on the three-inch rifle was then struck with an inspiration. The ground surrounding the fort had been cleared of trees for several hundred yards. This left hundreds of stumps dotting the landscape. The gunner took aim at one of the stumps on the eastern lip of the ravine. With an exploding percussion shell loaded, he pulled the lanyard, and the cannon barked to life. The gunner's aim was true, and the shell hit the stump. It exploded upon impact, sending a rain of deadly shrapnel in all directions, including down and into the face of those Confederates hugging the near wall of the ravine who could not be targeted directly. Although they could not tell from the fort, the effect was devastating to those seeking cover there. Shell after shell was fired into similar stumps, with comparable results.[183]

With Corse out of action, command of the fort, and of the whole garrison, fell to Colonel Rowett. Wanting to conserve ammunition, which was in short supply, and fearful of the Springfields overheating, he ordered the men to count off in relays. By readjusting, half the men could fire while the other half reloaded, much as they had when the battle began and they were three ranks deep. When the count ended, Rowett ordered a cease-fire. The rumor instantly began circulating that they were going to surrender. Adrenaline-fueled tempers flared, and those manning the western wall of the fort immediately turned their loaded rifles inward. They threatened to shoot the first man who raised a white flag and "clinched the threat with fearful oaths." Cries of "Never!" and "Die first!" filled the air. Colonel Rowett quickly dispelled the rumors and disavowed any intention to surrender. At that inopportune moment, a bullet took away part of his skull, putting him out of action for the battle. However, the cries to cease fire and the oaths denouncing surrender pulled Corse from his torpor. Although he had drifted in and out of consciousness and occasionally yelled or muttered something to try to encourage the men, for the most part he sat still. When he heard cries to cease fire and then surrender, he pulled himself together, jumped to his feet and shouted, "No surrender, hold Allatoona!" The shock must have

The Star Fort from the Confederates' point of view as they sought cover and shot at the defenders, outside the fort looking due east. *Photo by author.*

cleared his senses, for he was able to resume command of the garrison for the rest of the battle. His outburst did reopen his wound, and it had to be re-dressed.[184]

Try as they might, the Confederates couldn't close the distance and force their way into the fort. There is some disagreement as to how close the Rebels actually got. Alonzo R. Kibbe of the 12th Wisconsin Battery claimed that "the enemy did not get within several rods" of the fort. Many Confederates disagreed. French himself reported that they entered the ditch below the fort, but no Federal source confirms that fact. Ephraim Anderson in the 2nd and 6th Missouri said that they "advanced bravely and held their ground for some time at the very mouths of the cannon." Another Missourian said, "We got right up to it,—just a few steps away; and we trained our fire against the top of the works so that every time a Yankee put his head above the parapet about half a dozen men shot at him. We had the advantage of them, because we were lying down shooting up and they were raising up to shoot down."

The Confederate fire did have an effect. Both sides generally agree that eventually, probably at about noon, the fire from the fort began to slacken.

French believed that they had silenced the fort, and Captain Boyce of the 1st and 4th Missouri agreed. James H. Johnson, an aide to General Cockrell, rode his horse almost up to the northern wall. "I remember riding up very close to the fort," he later wrote, "though I am not able to say just how many yards it was; but the distance was short, as I was close enough to tell what the Federals were doing inside there." This may or may not be true, but the fire from the fort never totally ceased. Still, as even Corse admitted, "The gallant fellows struggled hard to keep their heads above the ditch and parapet in the face of the murderous fire of the enemy now concentrated upon us."[185]

The truth is that both sides were deadlocked. The Federals in the fort clung to the inner walls of the parapet, only occasionally rising to fire. When they did, they were met with a torrent of bullets. On the other hand, even if the Rebels had completely silenced the fort and could move around with relative impunity, it would take a full-scale assault to pry the Federals from their works, something they had already tried four times in the last hour and failed.

Alarmingly, ammunition for the cannons was running low, if not outright exhausted. The fire from the big guns had been a major deterrent and a big factor in the Confederate repulses. Remembering the cache of ammunition located across the cut, calls went out for volunteers to retrieve it. The shortest way to the ammunition was across the narrow footbridge ninety-five feet above the tracks, fully exposed to enemy fire. Several brave men rose to the occasion. One of them was Edwin R. Fullington, a member of the battery. He ran across the bridge, gathered an armload of artillery ammunition and returned to the Star Fort, all the while being shot at by the Confederates. Amazingly, he did this three times. Another volunteer was Frank Murphy of the 57th Illinois. He, too, braved the danger and returned with an armful of ammunition. Not all the volunteers were as lucky. Two men from the 93rd volunteered for the dangerous assignment and made their way across and to the cache. On the way back, one was shot, and he fell to his death. When they found him after the battle, he was still clutching the cartridges where he lay, a mangled and lifeless body on the iron rails.[186]

Still, morale began to ebb. The men in the fort were hot, tired and thirsty. Officer casualties were high. Corse and Rowett had both been wounded, several regimental commanders were gone and many company-level officers had fallen. A Minié ball shattered Lieutenant Amsden's leg below the knee while he was commanding the battery. Adding to their discomfort, there was no water other than what they had in their canteens. Yet it was the small things that kept them going. One regimental flag had been planted on the parapet. Throughout the fight, the staff had been shot away, but it had always been restored. Once again, a lead Rebel messenger struck down the symbol of the Union, and it fell into the dirt. Again cries of "Surrender" came from a few parched and demoralized throats, but one brave man leapt on the parapet amid a hail of bullets. He grasped the remnants of the staff, jammed it down into the earth once more and then dropped back to shelter unhurt. A great cheer erupted from the men.[187]

It was about one o'clock in the afternoon, and French had let the battle continue for about an hour since receiving Armstrong's last message. An hour's worth of attacks on the fort had failed to break the defenders' hold. The battle had settled into a stalemate. Unfortunately, time was working against French, and stalemate was an unacceptable outcome. With the limited information he had available, he had to assume the worst. A good general has to think of what the enemy might do, and the most logical course of action for Sherman was to cut French off from the rest of the army at Lost Mountain. He had a report from his cavalry stating that infantry were advancing north up the railroad. If he didn't want to risk isolation and capture, he would have to act now.

Other factors influenced his decision. His men were almost out of ammunition. It would take time to get more of it from the supply train on the ridge to the south, haul it up to the men and distribute it to the ranks. Again, time was something French no longer had. The men had been awake almost continually since the morning of the third, with only brief rests and naps. The men were near the limits of their endurance. Finally, his route back to the rest of the Army of Tennessee had to be taken into consideration. On a map, it looks easy enough to just go west along the Etowah and then south toward Burnt Hickory and then Lost Mountain. Unfortunately, an infantry division is not made up solely of men traveling by foot. It is supported by scores of wagons carrying munitions and food and ambulances transporting the wounded, not to mention the artillery that provides the hard-hitting fire support. These wheeled vehicles require passable roads. Regrettably, the road to the west traveled but a few yards from the Star Fort, which was still in the hands of the Federals, and quite literally under the guns of the enemy. There was no road connecting the supply train's position on the ridge near Moore's Hill and the Cartersville Road west of the garrison. French asked his young guide if there was another route they could take to reach New Hope Church. The guide replied that there was none. The only road to safety was the road on which they had arrived. With a heavy heart, French decided to call off the attack.[188]

When he informed his officers, they balked. Both Cockrell and Young stated that their men were "mad, and wanted to remain and capture the place." Captain Patrick Caniff, commanding the 3rd and 5th Missouri after the wounding of Major Waddell, and Colonel Garland of the 1st and 4th were both eager to continue. Colonel Elijah Gates of the 1st and 3rd Missouri Cavalry declared that he could capture the Star Fort in twenty minutes through the sally port after his men received more ammunition. There simply wasn't enough time to do so. They had failed and would have to begin their trek back to the army before they were cut off.[189]

Chapter 14

Tell My Wife I Loved Her to the Last

G eneral French began the process for an orderly withdrawal. Although he didn't record when he ordered the withdrawal to begin, it must have been just prior to or around one o'clock in the afternoon. Even before he made up his mind to disengage the infantry, he ordered Major Myrick to send two of the batteries and the artillery caissons south to act in concert with the 4th Mississippi besieging the blockhouse. It had been a long day for the cannoneers. Sergeant Caesar Landry of the Pointe Coupee Artillery wrote in his diary, "Our artillery done good execution. Our battery fired some 150 rounds, after a hot contest of about three hours our forces withdrew. We captured about 200 prisoners; our loss estimated between 600 & 900 killed, wounded and missing." After he had made the decision to leave, French sent a message to Sears with orders instructing the Mississippian to extricate himself and meet them on the ridge at their starting point. Finally, he ordered Cockrell and Young to begin pulling the men away from the battlefield, starting at 1:30 p.m. They would retire west and re-form where they had begun five hours earlier.[190]

The withdrawal of Ector and Cockrell's brigades was accomplished fairly easily. As described by French, the men in the two brigades "came out in squads, or individually." Once out of close range, they fell back and gathered underneath the shade of the trees at their starting point. Cockrell deployed skirmishers near Rowett's Redoubt, instructing them to keep up a constant fire and to cheer.[191]

Sears's Mississippians had the longest journey and the most difficult route to return. They had to gather themselves, skirt the millpond again and then turn south. They succeeded fairly well, although the last of them didn't stagger into the division assembly area until about three o'clock. William Chambers was among them. After resting shortly, he began making his way to the rear. On the way, he encountered Colonel William S. Barry and his 35th Mississippi. Barry had been wounded himself, his arm in a sling. "Sergeant, are you hurt?" asked the colonel. "A little," replied Chambers. "The rascals have shot my shoulder all to pieces." Passing on, others asked him about his injury. Eventually, he made his way to a makeshift surgeon's post, possibly where the division was gathering for the retreat. Somebody removed his coat, and Chambers saw for the first time that his sleeve was full of blood. The doctor there told him that he would have to go to the division hospital, located with the rest of the division's wagons and baggage train, to have the ball removed.[192]

Another group did its best to recover Colonel Clark. When the firing from the Star Fort was at a low ebb, three men from the regiment managed to drag the colonel to safety with a litter. As they made their way down the slope and out of harm's way, they enlisted the help of Private George G. Dillard of the 35th Mississippi. When the brigade withdrew to rejoin French, Dillard helped carry the colonel by having men take turns. When they arrived at the assembly area, Dillard had Assistant Sergeant A.R. Canfield of the 35th examine the wound and administer a stimulant. Dillard then secured a better litter for the journey south to the ambulances.[193]

Having had control of the village west of the railroad tracks for the past few hours, the warehouse containing the rations on the west side would have been easily visible to the Rebels there. It must have been maddening for these tired and hungry Confederates to realize that mountains of food were within arm's reach. Now that they had to leave, there would be no way to fill up wagonloads of it or even carry it off. However, if they couldn't take it, they had to destroy it. Various attempts were made to do so. An impressive story, from Henry Trimble's history of the 93rd Illinois, had one hundred men led by a lieutenant colonel rush the village in a flying column, only to be dispersed by well-directed volleys from the heights above, killing at least forty and wounding more. The rumored involvement of a high-ranking officer reached the 39th Iowa's Elisha Starbuck, who related that a lieutenant colonel was shot in the attempt. Unfortunately, no Confederate colonels, full bird or otherwise, were reported killed, captured or wounded anywhere near the village. And the 93rd history is the only one mentioning a grand column.[194]

Still, many stories of Confederates trying to burn the warehouses survive, so attempts were indeed made but probably on a smaller scale. The 4th

Minnesota's history notes that a Rebel lieutenant, "maddened at their frequent repulses," seized a firebrand and rushed from a house in the village toward the ration sheds. A marksman, possibly from Company E overlooking the village, put a bullet through the center of his forehead. This is somewhat corroborated by William Powers. After the battle, he "saw a dead rebel near the store-house, who had a fire-brand to burn our hard tack; under his outer suit was a Lieutenant's uniform, and there was taken from him a gold watch. On the east side of the shed where the crackers were stored, I saw a dead rebel and by him were splinters and matches, showing their determination to burn, if they could not capture the rations." In another story, a group of Rebels made it to the sheds. One broke down a door but was immediately felled with an axe in the hands of Tourtellotte's ubiquitous servant. If true, this noncombatant was one of the unsung, hardest-working defenders of the pass. The others were killed either in or around the shed. In all likelihood, individuals and even groups did try to burn the sheds in some force. Fortunately for the garrison and Sherman, none succeeded.[195]

The fate of the Mississippians trapped in the ravine below Company A was only slightly less grim, or at least, less fatal. Once it became clear that the rest of the brigade had withdrawn and that there was no hope of escape, eighty men of the 35th and 39th Mississippi raised the white flag. Members of both Company A and H descended to receive the surrender. Captain Edward U. Russell of Company A detailed Orderly Sergeant Thomas M. Young to take twenty men down into the ravine to collect the prisoners as well. They did so, and Young picked up one of the Mississippi flags and handed it to another soldier; they both proceeded to headquarters with their prize. Coming from the east, the members of Company H took their share of prizes. Merrit W. Cunningham received the sword of a Confederate officer, who also told him where to find his regimental flag. Also among the captured was Major Robert J. Durr, commanding officer of the 39th. It was he who had begun the day talking with Captain Morrill on the skirmish line during the truce.[196]

Back with the division, preparations continued for the withdrawal. The Federals inside the Star Fort kept up a desultory fire, and the Rebels weren't completely safe. As French surveyed the scene, a nearby soldier was walking back and forth "proudly displaying a pair of splendid new boots which he had gotten in the store house." A shot rang out from the fort, and the man fell dead at the commanding general's feet, the last man killed at Allatoona. The wounded had been brought to a spring near the ridge. Those who could not be carried and who could not walk themselves would have to be left behind. There was

Looking south into the ravine, where about eighty members of the 35th and 39th Mississippi were captured along with their battle flags. *Photo by author.*

no path, road or trail that could convey the ambulances from the ridge south to their position. French walked among them, explained why they had to be left and informed them that surgeons had been detailed to remain behind and care for them. As the men said their goodbyes to their comrades, Lieutenant Warren stopped by the field hospital to visit Major Waddell, who had been shot in the abdomen and comatose; a doctor informed Warren that there was no hope for the major. "I wanted to speak to him the parting word, but he was in a comatose condition, perfectly still. I could only look at him through blinding tears, press his lifeless hand and leave him," recalled the lieutenant. Henry Pool, shot between the eyes in the earlier assault, refused to be left behind. He convinced some of his friends to help carry him down the ridge to the ambulances. After the last of Sears' Brigade arrived at about three o'clock, the division began the short journey to the ridge south and the division wagons.[197]

William Chambers went with them but suffered several fainting spells along the way. When they finally gained the ridge near Moore's Hill, he found that he could not walk another step. Fearing that he would be left behind, he caught the attention of Lieutenant McLaurin and asked him to write a letter to his father informing him of his fate. At about that time, however, a teamster called out, "We can take one more wounded man from Sears' Brigade." "Here he is," answered McLaurin, and the lieutenant and others helped Chambers into the wagon. After a long day, his "share of that breakfast" was finally over.[198]

George Dillard began his trip with Colonel Clark, but the move proved too much for the wounded officer. "I placed him on the litter and started with him," wrote Dillard, "but he suffered so much pain on being moved and sank so fast, I abandoned the idea." Dillard had the men place Clark in a secure location, out of the way of passersby. A young soldier named Gardner from the 46th volunteered to remain with the colonel until the end. Clark's horse, sword, pistol, spurs and watch were entrusted to his body servant, a young slave from his plantation. Beckoning Dillard to his side, Clark conveyed some of his last words in broken whispers. "Tell my wife I loved her to the last. I have done my duty to my country, that I fell at my post, that I want my children to remember me." With that, Dillard left the colonel and moved to catch up to the division.[199]

Shortly after 3:30 p.m., French ordered Cockrell to take the infantry and join Colonel Thomas N. Adaire and his 4th Mississippi at the railroad bridge. The major general remained behind to see to the last of his men. He rode to the artillery position on Moore's Hill and there ordered Kolb's Battery to limber up and follow the division. French also ordered Colonel Andrews, the 39th North Carolina and the 32nd Texas Cavalry to form the rear guard and follow at about 5:00 p.m., Colonel Coleman and his small detachment having already withdrawn from the village and returned to the skirmish line. French was quite taken by the scene and the emotions it invoked, writing eloquently years later in his memoirs, "The declining sun, seen through the calm, hazy atmosphere, shone red, like the rising of the full-orbed moon, on the fortifications before us. All was silent now where the battle raged so long, and the mellow light gleamed so gently down on the wounded and the dead that I remarked to the officers and men around me: 'Silence, like the pall of death, rests over Allatoona; it is as lifeless as a graveyard at midnight.'" Shortly after four o'clock, French turned his horse and rode to catch up with the division.[200]

Lieutenant Fish had been trying to signal Allatoona all day. At 4:15 p.m., the smoke cleared enough that he tried again. This time the message went through:

We still hold out. General Corse is wounded.

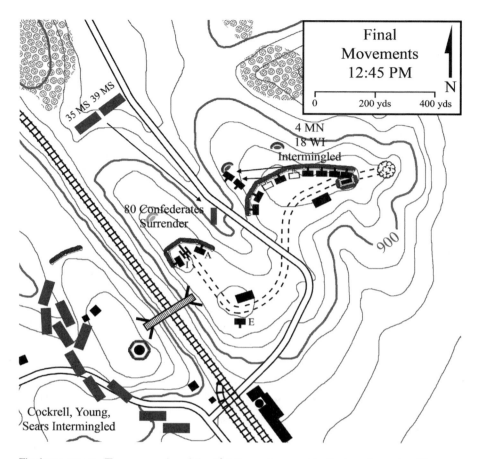

Final movements. Two companies of the 4th Minnesota moved to fire into the ravine. The Confederates nearly surrounded the Star Fort but could not capture it. *Courtesy of the author.*

West and McKenzie were no longer on signal duty, so the job of waving the flags and responding fell to R.O. McGinty and A.F. Fuller. Colonel Andrews's skirmishers were still down below near the village, so the work was not entirely without risk. Shortly, a series of messages flew between the two stations:

We are all right so far. General Corse is wounded. Where is General Sherman?

ADAMS, Signal Officer.

"Near you," was the curt response. However, Fish and his men then sent a longer message:

Tell Allatoona hold on. General Sherman says he is working hard for you.

The messages helped boost the morale of the exhausted outpost. Charles F. Hubert of the 50th Illinois later wrote, "These messages were soul stirring then, and to many souls the world over have been inspired since."[201]

General French soon overtook his division at the railroad bridge. There his men were engaged in capturing the stout wooden blockhouse that guarded the structure. Colonel Adaire and his Mississippians had already burned the wooden railroad trestle, more than two hundred feet long, as well as a new replacement that was already framed and almost ready for use. The blockhouse proved more resilient. Located south of the tracks and west of the creek, it rested on a small shelf above the stream. It had held out since the previous evening and proved impervious to the fire of the Mississippians' rifles and the lone cannon left behind to subdue it. With the arrival of the whole division and the remainder of Myrick's artillery battalion, the Confederates were able to bring all twelve tubes to bear on the little fort. In all, at least forty-nine rounds were fired at it, doing little damage. However, it did catch the wooden structure on fire. This ultimately proved to be the undoing of the brave Wisconsin men. The smoke and heat were too much and forced the capitulation of the stalwart defenders.[202]

The Badger State men soon mingled with their captors. Captain Boyce of Missouri struck up a conversation with Captain O'Brien and had quite a laugh at Captain Luman N. Carpenter of Company E. Carpenter had only recently received his captain's commission and, with it, a new uniform. He had only donned the new clothes the previous day.

"It's a shame," said O'Brien, "to send a man to prison who is as nicely dressed as Carpenter."

"O'Brien, it's all right for you," replied Carpenter, "as your clothes are not much account anyhow, and you have been a captain for some time; but just think of my case; I am so well fixed up that really I hate to sit down anyhow. If I had my old clothes on I wouldn't feel so bad about it." To Boyce he said, "Boyce, that's mighty poor cooking you have got in your haversack. If you fellows had gone into this fight for grub, instead of blood and prisoners, you would have a damn sight better spread to offer your unwilling guests." After exchanging their worn-out rifles for those just surrendered, the eighty-two officers and men marched into captivity.[203]

The Confederates began the long march back to New Hope Church. After a tedious trip, they ended their long journey at midnight at the residence of Dr. Augustus Smith. The moon briefly appeared near nightfall, but gathering clouds and the rumble of thunder heralded a storm. After a short rest, the division resumed its journey and safely entered friendly lines the next morning. French immediately called on General Hood at his headquarters. He found his commanding officer in a gloomy mood:

> *Hood reminded me of a disheartened man. His countenance was sad and his voice doleful. He received me with a melancholy air, and asked no questions; did not refer to the battle, "told me where my corps was, and said he would leave next day." He seemed much depressed in spirits.*[204]

With that, the odyssey of French and his men came to an end. They had marched hard, destroyed several miles of railroad and assaulted a fortified enemy position. They had come within a hair's breadth of succeeding. In the end, all they could bring away from the journey was the satisfaction of miles of twisted rail ties and the memory of those they had left behind. The Union war effort could easily repair the tracks, but the loss of friends and comrades would stay with them a lifetime.

Chapter 15

The Enemy Suffered Very Severely

As Colonel Andrews's men, the last of French's Division to leave the field, marched away toward the blockhouse, the garrison began to collect itself. The most urgent task was the need to locate the wounded and help those who had a chance of surviving. In doing so, the defenders came face to face with the grim cost of the battle. Crushed and twisted bodies lay everywhere. The ravine to the northwest of the Star Fort in particular proved a ghastly sight. Occupied for hours during the battle and used as a staging ground for the final attacks against the fort, it was subject to an intense fire by both infantry rifles and cannons. As Henry Trimble wrote after the war, "The scene in that ravine, after the battle was ended, was beyond all powers of description. All the languages of earth combined are inadequate to tell half its horrors. Mangled and torn in every conceivable manner, the dead and wounded were everywhere, in heaps and windrows."[205]

The tent of the 93rd Illinois' adjutant stood as mute testimony to the ferocity of the gunfire. A large wall tent, it had four-foot vertical walls and was held up by an eight-foot vertical pole in the center. Located in the space between the fort and the ravine, it had been all but shredded. Thirteen of the sixteen ropes that held it to the ground were severed. Of the vertical walls, "not a single square inch in either wall of the tent that had not been penetrated by one or more bullets." Yet the sloped top was mostly intact, with several feet not having a single bullet hole or tear. The fire had been so intense and so low to the ground, both firing up from the edge of the ravine toward the fort and down into the ravine by the defenders, that the upper half was largely spared.[206]

Bodies lay everywhere. "After the skirmish I walked out over the battlefield," wrote a survivor after the war, "and I can safely say that anywhere north and west of the west front, a man could have walked from thirty to two hundred yards, had he felt so inclined, without stepping off from the bodies of the dead and wounded rebels."[207]

The greatest horrors awaited them at Rowett's Redoubt. Bodies, both living and dead, littered the ground. Even the veterans with more than three years of war under their belt were appalled. One wrote, "There was the only place in four years' service under Grant, McPherson, Sherman and Logan, where I saw the blood run along the ground. In the road at that redoubt the dust was several inches deep, and along in that dust a rivulet of purple ran for six or eight rods, and one hundred and sixteen soldiers of the blue and gray lay dead in one heap on less than an eighth of an acre of ground."[208]

Captain Smith of the 7th Illinois returned to the redoubt after the battle to collect the dead. There, in a deep wagon rut in the old road, he found the body of William Burwell. He lay facedown, with Smith's silver-plated Henry rifle underneath and covered in his blood. Smith recovered the weapon, although sixteen other Henrys in his company were missing and presumably fell into Confederate hands.[209]

Others took stock of just how close the battle had been. Lieutenant Ludlow noted that of the 165,000 rounds of ammunition that Corse had brought with the brigade, only 250 remained when the battle was over. Other mementos gave mute testimony to the savage fighting. The 12th Wisconsin Battery had only recently received a new flag shortly before the battle. By the end, the men counted 192 holes, courtesy of enemy bullets.[210]

Help finally arrived later in the evening. Lieutenant Colonel Hurlbut and his small command rode into the station on their small train at about 8:00 p.m. Upon arrival, he found out that he was the highest ranking unwounded officer present from the Third Brigade and assumed command of the unit. The train also brought General Raum to the pass. He found Corse, Tourtellotte and Rowett together in a house, along with Lieutenant Amsden. The general was present when the surgeons removed the lieutenant's leg. When the train returned north that night, Raum was on board. Once at Cartersville, he wired a message to General Smith at Chattanooga:[211]

We have won a great victory at Allatoona to-day. I am just from there. General Corse slightly wounded in cheek; Colonel Tourtellotte slightly in left thigh;

View of the battlefield in 1938 from the Cartersville Road just behind Rowett's Redoubt. The Star Fort is on the hill in the background. *Atlanta History Center, VIS 197.259.09.*

Major Fisher also wounded. Our loss about 100 killed and 200 wounded. The enemy suffered very severely, and have retreated toward Dallas. The Rebel surgeons have surrendered their hospitals. Lieutenant Amsden loses a leg, broken below knee. General Sherman has been fighting to-day.[212]

These would be the only reinforcements to arrive that day. The three Union armies were in a long arc, with Howard on the left near Kolb's Farm, Stanley in the center at Pine Mountain and Little Kennesaw and Cox on the ridge one mile north of Kennesaw itself. Kilpatrick's cavalry was coordinating with Howard, and Garrard was west of Pine Mountain. In fact, when Sherman received the news that Allatoona still held, he had Elliott hold off sending Garrard's division to Allatoona. Instead, he issued orders for the next day to move the division toward New Hope Church and gather information on the enemy there. Sherman did, however, suggest sending one squadron of horsemen to the pass to open communications.[213]

At Allatoona, the survivors took the wounded to hastily arranged field hospitals. The Clayton House, located in the village, was one building taken over for that purpose. So was the headquarters building of the 4th Minnesota. Any structure that could house and shelter casualties was appropriated. Rebel surgeons, left behind, helped tend to their own wounded. Into the evening and all night long, the doctors applied scalpel, clamp and saw to treat their patients. During the night, the light of their flickering candles was augmented by brief flashes of lightning. The rains soon followed and continued several hours past dawn. A new day brought a sight never forgotten. "All around the house shown in the cut of Allatoona, lay the dead, dying and wounded, waiting to be borne, some to their last resting place, some to the amputating table, and others to the care of their comrades."[214]

The final cost was staggering. Of the 2,190 Union officers and men present 707, or 32 percent, became casualties. Of these, 142 were killed, 353 wounded and 212 missing in action. This includes the fight at the blockhouse guarding the railroad bridge. In addition, there were few, if any, military noncombatants, and if Tourtellotte is to be believed, several civilians took up arms as well. Those are hefty casualties for a small, division-sized engagement. For comparison, the Union incurred a 21 percent casualty rate at Shiloh, 27 percent at Gettysburg and, more closely, 31 percent at Stone's River. Nearly all of the officers in charge were wounded to some degree, including Corse, Rowett, Tourtellotte, Redfield, Hanna and Fisher. The 39th Iowa was mauled. Of the 284 officers and men it began the day with, 170 were out of action by the end, counting 40 dead, 52 wounded and 78 missing. With 60 percent of its men casualties, it had both the highest percentage and highest total loss among all Union regiments. The 7th Illinois was a close second, losing 141 men out of 313 in the battle, for a total percentage of 45 percent. The losses of these two units underscores the viciousness of the fighting at Rowett's Redoubt. On the other side of the spectrum, the large 4th Minnesota was easily able to absorb the 44 men it lost, suffering only 9 percent overall.[215]

Confederate losses were even higher. French's Division could count about 3,553 present during the battle, including the artillery. Even this is probably exaggerated, since the number is taken from the division's September 20 returns. It doesn't take into account any straggling that would have occurred during the march from the Chattahoochee, the marathon exertion of reaching to the Western & Atlantic Railroad and destroying it and then moving north to Allatoona—all within about forty-four hours and with little or no sleep. Additionally, to give a fair comparison to the Union losses, the noncombatants have to be excluded. This would include the teamsters driving the wagons, the two regiments guarding the artillery on Moore's Hill and anybody else not directly engaged in the battle. According to French, it was a little over 2,000 men and was probably closer to about 2,250. French reported 898 casualties, consisting of 134 killed, 474 wounded and 290 missing. This yields a percentage loss of 40 percent. In contrast, Lee lost 29 percent of his army at Chancellorsville and 37 percent at Gettysburg. Like their northern opponents, officer casualties were high. General Young was wounded, two regimental commanders were mortally wounded, two more were wounded but survived and one was captured. A number of other field and line officers were also injured. Cockrell's Brigade lost 271 men, or 26 percent, while Ector's Brigade lost 201, which equates to 50 percent. By far, Sears' Brigade lost the most. Of the nearly 800 men engaged, 425 of them were lost. Not surprisingly, 256 of those were listed as missing, most of whom were probably captured. By contrast, Cockrell reported only 22 missing and Young 11. The 35th and 39th Mississippi, facing long odds against the entrenched 4th Minnesota, suffered the highest number of casualties among the Confederates, with 147 and 112 men lost, respectively. The highest percentage loss recorded belonged to the 9th Texas. It began the battle with just 92 officers and men but lost 49 of them in the fight, a staggering 53 percent. Corse reported picking up eight hundred small arms. However, French noted that this was almost entirely because his men dropped their inferior and worn-out weapons and exchanged them for newer ones from the dead and wounded Federals.[216]

The next day began with an overcast sky and a dreary rain. The task of collecting and burying the dead continued. The men of the 93rd Illinois buried their dead on the crest of the ridge about two hundred feet southwest of the Star Fort. They were laid side by side in a common grave. After the trench was filled, each soldier received an individual headboard with his name, company and regiment carved into it. Other regiments followed suit. When the war ended, each would be disinterred and reburied at the National Cemetery in Marietta. The Confederate dead were also buried, but with much less fanfare. Many had been killed or crawled, after being mortally wounded, into the myriad hollows and crevices in the surrounding terrain. The last of the Rebel dead were not discovered and buried until October 22.

Reinforcements converged on the pass. At ten o'clock that morning, Lieutenant Colonel Roger Martin and the First Brigade of Corse's division arrived. Corse now had three brigades at Allatoona, two of his and Tourtellotte's from Raum's division. His last brigade remained at Rome.[217]

Armstrong's cavalry was still north of Marietta, so the telegraphs were still out and signaling was the only way to relay messages between Sherman, Allatoona and points north. At 2:30 p.m., Lieutenant Fish received the following message from Corse at Allatoona:

Where is General Sherman? Have you any news from him?

Sherman soon responded, having his message relayed from Marietta:

Am Reconnoitering toward Burnt Hickory and Lost Mountain. Are you badly wounded? If all is right at Allatoona I want you back at Rome.

At 3:15 p.m., Corse sent the following message, full of his usual bluster:

I am short a cheek bone and one ear, but am able to whip all hell yet. My losses are very heavy. A force moving from Stilesborough on Kingston gives me some anxiety. Tell me where Sherman is?

Sherman's aide-de-camp, Captain L.M. Dayton, responded for the general:

Saw your battle. Am here all right. Have sent you assistance. Am sorry you are hurt. General is mindful of you.

Sherman himself arrived at the top of the mountain at 6:45 p.m. and sent a message himself:

Am just in. Am very sorry at your wound; but all is right with you. If possible, keep the enemy off your lines, and let me know at once what force you have and what is at Kingston and Rome; also signal some account of your fight. Hood has retreated to Dallas.[218]

With that, Sherman turned his attention to larger matters. Hood had retired from Lost Mountain during the day and had moved his army west toward Dallas and New Hope Church. Fearing for the safety of the Etowah River crossings, Sherman ordered Corse at 9:30 p.m. to move his command back to Rome the next morning. He also ordered General Cox to have a brigade ready to move toward Allatoona at first light. Corse began withdrawing his men from Allatoona early on the morning of the seventh, and Colonel Casement's brigade from the Twenty-third Corps arrived that afternoon. Allatoona was secure.[219]

Sherman admired generals who fought and wanted other garrisons along the line to follow Corse's example. In Sherman's words, he "esteemed this defense of Allatoona so handsome and important" that he issued General Order No. 86 on October 7:

The general commanding avails himself of the opportunity, in the handsome defense made of Allatoona, to illustrate the most important principle in war, that fortified posts should be defended to the last, regardless of the relative numbers of the party attacking and attacked...

The thanks of this army are due and are hereby accorded to General Corse, Colonel Tourtellotte, Colonel Rowett, officers, and men, for their determined and gallant defense of Allatoona, and it is made an example to illustrate the importance of preparing in time, and meeting the danger, when present, boldly, manfully, and well.

Commanders and garrisons of the posts along our railroad are hereby instructed that they must hold their posts to the last minute, sure that the time gained is valuable and necessary to their comrades at the front.[220]

Sherman met with Corse a few days later and came face to face with one of the young brigadier's "exaggerations." He was surprised to find on his cheek a small bandage. When Corse removed it, Sherman saw a mere scratch on his cheek, as well as no damage to the ear he had claimed to have lost. Laughing, Sherman told him, "Corse, they came damn near to missing you, didn't they?"[221]

Hood's campaign against Sherman's supply lines continued. Making his way north, Hood eventually engaged other outposts along the railroad at Resaca and Dalton, the latter of which surrendered to the Confederates on the fourteenth. Sherman and his armies followed, but Hood declined to give the decisive battle he had espoused to President Davis. Instead he retired to Gadsden, Alabama, arriving there on the twentieth. Sherman followed but did not pursue vigorously. Instead, he kept his forces at arm's length. When Hood continued north, Sherman returned to Atlanta in early November. The stage was set for two final campaigns: Hood into Tennessee and Sherman through Georgia and the Carolinas.[222]

The public's attention shifted to other fields of battle, but the struggle for Allatoona was not forgotten by the men who fought there. Union veterans remembered the battle with a sense of pride. The men of the 7th Illinois, in particular, held their participation in the battle in high esteem. Their postwar reunions were full of anecdotes and remembrances of their fight at Rowett's Redoubt. For the Confederates, Allatoona was a lost opportunity. Many believed that if they had captured the garrison or destroyed the rations stored there, the subsequent March to the Sea could have been averted. Unfortunately, this was not the case. Not every battle is going to change the course of the war, and some serve no purpose other than to wear down the enemy's will and capacity to resist. The railroads that Hood's men destroyed were repaired, and Slocum in Atlanta foraged and gathered more than enough supplies from the surrounding civilian population to feed Sherman's armies. The Union war machine could make up the losses in men and matériel; the Confederacy could not. No more Texans and Missourians were going to come across the Mississippi River to bolster the ranks of Cockrell and Young, and the prospects of more Mississippians joining Sears were slim.

What the battle did display was the superb fighting qualities of the men and women involved. At least one Missouri woman, not content to sit by while her kinsmen fought at the front, joined the cause and fought for their independence. At least two black men, though civilians, participated when given a chance to fight for their freedom and survival, apparently with a will. The Union defenders gave their all for the defense of the garrison, and their Confederate opponents did likewise, very nearly gaining the upper hand and achieving victory. However, in the end, the fight did little to change the course of the war. It was, as General French so eloquently put to paper in the midst of the battle, a "needless effusion of blood."[223]

Appendix A

Grave of the Unknown Soldier

A t the current intersection of Old Allatoona Road and Oak Hollow Road south of Allatoona Pass lies a lonely grave. A sign above it reads simply, "An Unknown Hero." A small, marble headstone reads:

The grave of the "Unknown Hero" at Allatoona Pass in its modern location. *Photo by author.*

An Unknown Hero.
He Died for the Cause
He thought was Right.

Once located on the battlefield itself, the grave has since been moved to its present location. He could have been a soldier in the 35th Mississippi who was initially buried where he fell. He could have also been a Confederate whose body was shipped back to the pass several days after the battle. We may never know for certain. Whether he is a Confederate or Federal, he remains one of the thousands of "Unknown Soldiers" who have fallen in our nation's wars. As such, as an American, he deserves the respect and honor due all our fellow countrymen who have perished in battle, regardless of the politics of the era.

Appendix B

The Allatoona Blockhouse

The fight for the blockhouse guarding the railroad bridge over Allatoona Creek is often overlooked. It's a fascinating story. Eighty-two men trapped in a wooden fort, outnumbered forty-one to one. Their stubborn resistance caused French to leave behind a regiment from Sears' Brigade and a cannon to engage the fort. Could one more regiment in the brigade have helped even the odds against the 4th Minnesota or provided the final impetus needed to overwhelm the Star Fort? In the end, it took the return of the rest of the division and the concentrated firepower of the entire artillery battalion to force its surrender.

The blockhouse was located on a shelf above Allatoona Creek. This shelf was on the west side of the stream and south of the tracks of the Western & Atlantic Railroad. In a straight line, it was about 300 to 350 feet from the blockhouse to the bridge. The fort itself was about 30 feet wide by 42 feet long. It was constructed like a stockade. The men dug a trench, stood the timbers upright and filled in the trench with the dirt. The earth was banked against the timbers on the outside walls of the structure. Apertures could then be cut to provide fields of fire. It proved remarkably resilient to damage. The garrison only surrendered when enemy artillery caught the roof on fire.

After the war, the location of the blockhouse, and the story behind it, was largely forgotten. On April 12, 1947, noted Atlanta historian Wilbur Kurtz and his companion Colonel Thomas Spencer journeyed from Atlanta to the area to find the blockhouse. They found it rather easily and mapped its location relative to the railroad bridge, nearby roads and Allatoona Creek. They also

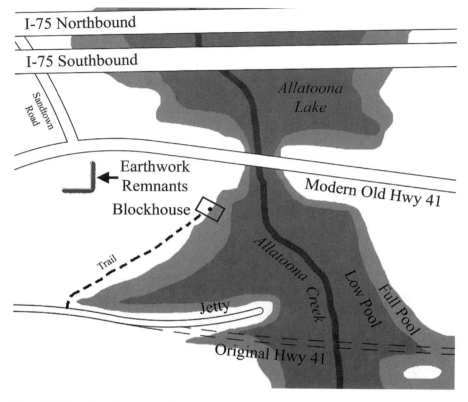

Map of the location of the Allatoona blockhouse. The full and low waterlines for Allatoona Lake are shown. The railroad followed modern Old Highway 41. *Courtesy of the author.*

discovered the remnants of other nearby earthworks. Kurtz took extensive notes in his journal and photographed the area relative to the bridge.[224]

Much has changed since that visit—unfortunately for the blockhouse, not for the better. Allatoona Creek was dammed, and flooding began in late December 1949. Grading for Allatoona Lake destroyed the shelf on which the blockhouse stood, and at full capacity, the lake covers the most of the location. However, when the lake levels are low, one can stand in the approximate location of the old fort. The creation of the lake also necessitated the rerouting of the railroad. Instead of the large curve south of Allatoona, the railroad now goes straight from Acworth to just south of the pass, more or less following the old direct road that Captain Jackson defended in the dead of night on October 4, 1864. It then curves west, and it no longer travels through the cut. The old railroad bed is now used as the path for the current Sandtown Road SE/Allatoona Pass Road SE. The railroad bridge at the site of the blockhouse now carries Old Highway 41, and the dual bridge carrying Interstate 75 lies just north of it. The original US Highway 41 at the bridge is now underwater. Part of it forms a jetty that extends into the lake and is used for recreational fishing.

Access to the location of the former blockhouse is easy. From Acworth, take North Main Street/Old US Highway 41 north. After the road crosses the lake, take the next left, which is labeled as a "Boat Ramp." This is actually the original Highway 41 before the rising lake waters submerged the roadway. Park at the recreational area and walk toward the jetty until you come to the old trail just north of the lakeshore. Follow this path, and it will take you to the shore at the approximate location of the old blockhouse. From the battlefield park, drive down Old Allatoona Road. The road will change names to Allatoona Pass Road and then to Sandtown Road. The road ends at Old Highway 41. Turn right, and the "Boat Ramp" is the next left.

Order of Battle

The Order of Battle in the following pages lists the units present at the Battle of Allatoona, and their strengths. Numbers in parentheses indicate estimates. Full explanations for individual units are given in their notes.

	Officers	Men
UNION	85	1,752

Army of the Tennessee
Brig. Gen. John M. Corse
(commanding forces at Allatoona Pass)

Staff		5

Fifteenth Army Corps
Third Division

	Officers	Men
First Brigade (Allatoona Garrison)	48	958
Lt. Col. John E. Tourtellotte		
18th Wisconsin[225]	(12)	228
93rd Illinois[226]	14	280
4th Minnesota[227]	(22)	450
5th Ohio Cavalry (detachment)[228]		
12th Wisconsin Battery[229]		

	Officers	Men
Fourth Division	37	789
Second Brigade (attached to 3rd Brigade)		
12th Illinois[230]	8	155

	Officers	Men
Third Brigade	29	634
Col. Richard Rowett		
7th Illinois[231]	(14)	299
50th Illinois[232]		
57th Illinois (Companies A and B)[233]	(5)	61
39th Iowa[234]	10	274

Strength	KIA	WIA	MIA	Total	%
2,190	142	353	212	707	32%
5		1		1	
1,092	39	113	94	246	23%
240	2	12	84	98	41%
294	21	52	10	83	28%
472	11	33		44	9%
15					
71	5	16		21	30%
1,093	103	239	118	460	42%
163	9	49		58	36%
930	94	190	118	402	43%
313	35	67	39	141	45%
267	15	63		78	29%
66	4	8	1	13	20%
284	40	52	78	170	60%

	Officers	Men
CONFEDERACY	339	3,214

Army of Tennessee
Stewart's Corps

French's Division[235]	329	2,962

Maj. Gen. Samuel G. French
Staff

Ector's Brigade[236]
Brig. Gen. William H. Young
10th Texas Cavalry (dismounted)

14th Texas Cavalry (dismounted)[237]	(5)	87

32nd Texas Cavalry (dismounted)
9th Texas[238]
29th North Carolina[239]
39th North Carolina[240]

Cockrell's Brigade[241]
Brig. Gen. Francis M. Cockrell
1st and 4th Missouri
2nd and 6th Missouri
3rd and 5th Missouri
1st and 3rd Missouri Cavalry (dismounted)

Sears' Brigade[242]
Brig. Gen. Claudius W. Sears
7th Mississippi Battalion

Strength	KIA	WIA	MIA	Total	%
3,553	134	474	290	898	25%
3,291	134	474	290	898	27%
(2,250)					40%
			1	1	
(400)	43	147	11	201	50%
92	4	45		49	53%
101				45	45%
138	12	39	3	54	39%
		2		2	
(1,050)	49	200	22	271	26%
	5	37	2	44	
	16	62	13	91	
	18	53	5	76	
	10	48	2	60	
(800)	42	127	256	425	53%
	1	13	16	30	

	Officers	Men

4th Mississippi

35th Mississippi

36th Mississippi

39th Mississippi

46th Mississippi

	Officers	Men
Artillery Battalion[243]	10	252

Maj. John D. Myrick

Pointe Coupée Louisiana Artillery

Barbour Alabama Battery

Brookhaven Mississippi Battery

Strength	KIA	WIA	MIA	Total	%
		4		4	
	12	52	83	147	
		8	24	32	
	11	24	77	112	
	18	26	56	100	

262

Notes

CHAPTER 1

1. Trimble, *History of the Ninety-third*, 124–25.
2. Ibid. 125.
3. Ludlow, *Battle of Allatoona*, 35–36.
4. Ibid., 36–37; Starbuck, "Hold the Fort."

CHAPTER 2

5. U.S. War Department, *War of the Rebellion: A Compilation of the Official Records of the Union and Confederate Armies*, series I, vol. 39, part I, 801 (hereafter cited as *Official Records*; all references are to series I unless otherwise indicated); Davis, *Rise and Fall*, 564–65.
6. Foster, *One of Cleburne's Command*, 130–31; *Official Records*, vol. 38, part V, 1,023–24; Hood, *Advance and Retreat*, 252–53.
7. Foster, *One of Cleburne's Command*, 135.
8. Hood, *Advance and Retreat*, 249–52; Sword, *Confederacy's Last Hurrah*, 36–37.

9. *Official Records*, vol. 39, part I, 805; Hood, *Advance and Retreat*, 254; Davis, *Rise and Fall*, 565.

10. Chambers, *Blood & Sacrifice*, 170; Patrick, *Reluctant Rebel*, 230; Hood, *Advance and Retreat*, 253.

11. Hood, *Advance and Retreat*, 254–55; *Official Records*, vol. 39, part I, 805.

12. *Official Records*, vol. 39, part II, 879–80.

CHAPTER 3

13. Davis, *Life of David Bell Birney*, 245.

14. Sherman, *Memoirs*, 134–35.

15. Castel, *Decision in the West*, 541–42; *Official Records*, vol. 38, part I, 82–83.

16. Sherman, *Memoirs*, 141; Woodworth, *Nothing but Victory*, 584; Ecelbarger, *Day Dixie Died*, 216–17; *Official Records*, vol. 39, part II, 440–41.

17. *Official Records*, vol. 39, part II, 355–56, 411–12, 480; Porter, *Campaigning with Grant*, 289–96.

18. *Official Records*, vol. 39, part II, 463, 465; Sherman, *Memoirs*, 141.

CHAPTER 4

19. Foster, *One of Cleburne's Command*, 135.

20. French, *Two Wars*, 2, 16–20, 80, 130, 132–33, 135, 183; Warner, *Generals in Gray*, 94.

21. Gottschalk, *In Deadly Earnest*, 342; *Official Records*, vol. 32, part III, 825, 828.

22. Gottschalk, *In Deadly Earnest*, 28–29, 57–70, 88–95, 139–45, 216–25, 251–57, 268–70, 365–70; *Official Records*, vol. 39, part II, 855.

23. Gottschalk, *In Deadly Earnest*, 326–28; Warner, *Generals in Gray*, 57.

24. *Official Records*, vol. 39, part II, 855; Stroud, *Ector's Texas Brigade*, 27–30, 39–41, 77–81, 99–108, 170; Powell, *Maps of Chickamauga*, 54–57.

25. Warner, *Generals in Gray*, 348–49; Stroud, *Ector's Texas Brigade*, 176.

26. *Official Records*, vol. 39, part II, 855; Newton, *Lost for the Cause*, 120–23.

27. Warner, *Generals in Gray*, 16, 271–72; Chambers, *Blood & Sacrifice*, 54.

28. *Official Records*, vol. 39, part II, 851.
29. Ibid., 850–51; Wheeler's Confederate Cavalry Association, *Campaigns of Wheeler*, 274.
30. Foster, *One of Cleburne's Command*, 135; Chambers, *Blood & Sacrifice*, 171; *Official Records*, vol. 39, part I, 806, 810.
31. *Official Records*, vol. 39, part I, 806; Chambers, *Blood & Sacrifice*, 171; French, *Two Wars*, 223.
32. French, *Two Wars*, 223–25. French and his memoirs are the only source for this meeting, so it's entirely possible that he wrote the encounter showing himself in the best possible light as the "voice of reason" decades after the fact.
33. Patrick, *Reluctant Rebel*, 231.
34. Gottschalk, *In Deadly Earnest*, 413.

Chapter 5

35. *Official Records*, vol. 39, part II, 525.
36. Ibid., part I, 633; part II, 521.
37. Ibid., part II, 526–27.
38. Raines, *Getting the Message Through*, 6–7.
39. *Official Records*, vol. 39, part I, 739; Fish, "Signal Corps," April 19, 1883.
40. *Official Records*, vol. 39, part I, 724; part II, 552–53; Warner, *Generals in Blue*, 266.
41. Evans, *Sherman's Horsemen*, 3, 203, 402; *Official Records*, vol. 39, part II, 442.
42. *Official Records*, vol. 39, part II, 518–20.
43. Ibid., part I, 728; part II, 533.
44. Ibid., part II, 532, 540, 542.
45. Ibid., part III, 3–4.
46. Ibid., 5–6.
47. Ibid., 6.
48. Ibid., 8–10.
49. Fish, "Signal Corps," April 19, 1883.
50. *Official Records*, vol. 39, part I, 591; part III, 9–10.

CHAPTER 6

51. Trimble, *History of the Ninety-third*, 102.

52. Scaife, *Allatoona Pass*, 14; Trimble, *History of the Ninety-third*, 102–103.

53. Castel, *Decision in the West*, 213–14; Sherman, *Memoirs*, 149; Brown, *History of the Fourth*, 307.

54. Trimble, *History of the Ninety-third*, 103, 106; Scaife, *Allatoona Pass*, 15.

55. Scaife, *Allatoona Pass*, 15.

56. Ibid., 16.

57. Trimble, *History of the Ninety-third*, 103, 106; Scaife, *Allatoona Pass*, 15.

58. Trimble, *History of the Ninety-third*, 106.

59. Trimble, *History of the Ninety-third*, 106; Scaife, *Allatoona Pass*, 15–16; Brown, *Battle of Allatoona*, 4.

60. Trimble, *History of the Ninety-third*, 107, 109; Brown, *Battle of Allatoona*, 4–6.

61. Trimble, *History of the Ninety-third*, 106, 120; Brown, *History of the Fourth*, 308; Scaife, *Allatoona Pass*, 15.

62. *Official Records*, vol. 39, part I, 748; Brown, *History of the Fourth*, 295, 301–302, 304; Aldrich, *Annals of Iowa*, 287. In a postwar letter, Colonel Tourtellotte mentioned to Corse that the 12th Wisconsin Battery was in the middle of a reorganization of the battery. It was due to turn in the rifled guns and re-form with all Napoleons. The men had been issued the Napoleons but had not yet turned in the rifles, giving the battery a total of eight cannons. This is the only mention of this fact. All other reports and eyewitness accounts give the battery having only six cannons. I decided to go with the preponderance of the evidence.

63. *Official Records*, vol. 39, part I, 751–52; Nanzig, *Badax Tigers*, 284; Chapman, *Roster of Wisconsin Volunteers*, 83–111. There is much confusion from multiple sources regarding which companies were detached and stationed at the blockhouse. A careful reading of the 18th Wisconsin's roster, however, reveals that Companies E, F and I had the vast majority of prisoners taken at Allatoona.

64. Brown, *History of the Fourth*, 37–38, 92–93, 119–26, 137, 140, 254, 575.

65. Laraba, "Graced the Captain's Table."

66. Trimble, *History of the Ninety-third*, 97–98.

CHAPTER 7

67. *Official Records*, vol. 39, part III, 782; Hood, *Advance and Retreat*, 256.

68. Foster, *One of Cleburne's Command*, 136; Patrick, *Reluctant Rebel*, 231–32.

69. *Official Records*, vol. 39, part I, 806; part III, 31–32, 783; French, *Two Wars*, 225.

70. Chambers, *Blood & Sacrifice*, 171; Patrick, *Reluctant Rebel*, 231.

71. Foster, *One of Cleburne's Command*, 136–37.

72. *Official Records*, vol. 39, part III, 783.

73. Ibid., part I, 788; part III, 29, 33, 780–81.

74. Ibid., part III, 27–28.

75. Ibid., 27, 29, 34.

76. Ibid., part I, 806, 812; Hood, *Advance and Retreat*, 256; Chambers, *Blood & Sacrifice*, 171; Kurtz, Notebook 20, 387, 412. "Cooley" is the correct spelling for the house at which the army headquarters ended the day. Hood and other Confederates in their reports and memoirs list it as the "Carley" house. However, the prominent Atlanta historian Wilbur Kurtz tracked down the house, as well as the correct spelling for the family name, based on church and burial records.

77. *Official Records*, vol. 39, part I, 812, 825; Lowry, "Taken in at Big Shanty"; French, *Two Wars*, 225; Chambers, *Blood & Sacrifice*, 171. Stewart reported capturing about one hundred men at Big Shanty. Both French and Chambers (based on his journal) state that forty prisoners were captured at Big Shanty. However, records show that Companies A and B were nearly at full strength with one hundred men each. Even taking into account those absent, assigned elsewhere or escaped, Stewart's total sounds more plausible, and neither French nor Chambers were actually at Big Shanty.

78. *Official Records*, vol. 39, part I, 812; Barber, *Army Memoirs*, 153, 158–60. Stewart reported capturing "a few hundred" men at Acworth. Barber stated that they had about 150.

79. *Official Records*, vol. 39, part I, 825; Boyce, *Captain Joseph Boyce*, 180; Chambers, *Blood & Sacrifice*, 172.

80. *Official Records*, vol. 39, part III, 46, 51–54.

81. Ibid., 43–45, 47–49, 75; Fish, "Signal Corps," April 19, 1883.

82. *Official Records*, vol. 39, part I, 814.

83. Jones, *Southern Historical Society Papers*, 405.

84. *Official Records*, vol. 39, part I, 814.

85. Ibid., 817, 821; part II, 858; Flatau, "Only Regiment of Confederate Artillery"; French, *Two Wars*, 234; Scaife, *Allatoona Pass*, 65. The composition of the artillery battalion is suspect and does not match up with

the September 20 returns. French mentions Captain Kolb by name in his official report. Colonel David Coleman of the 39th North Carolina likewise mentions the Pointe Coupée battery in his report. The identity of the third battery is somewhat of a mystery. L.S. Flatau mentions Allatoona Heights as one of the battery's engagements in a *Confederate Veteran* article and is the only confirmation among information on all possible candidates.

86. *Official Records*, vol. 39, part I, 615, 730, 790; part III, 65–66, 70.

87. Ibid., part I, 726; part III, 71, 75, 76.

88. Fish, "Signal Corps," April 19, 1883.

89. *Official Records*, vol. 39, part III, 77,78.

90. Ibid., 75.

91. Ibid., 78; Kirk, *History of the Fifteenth Pennsylvania*, 400; Frankenberry, "Visiting War Scenes."

92. French, *Two Wars*, 225. French says in his diary that they left Big Shanty at three o'clock in the afternoon, but his official report says 3:30 p.m.

CHAPTER 8

93. Castel, *Decision in the West*, 198.

94. Warner, *Generals in Blue*, 94.

95. Wright, *History of the Sixth Iowa*, 183.

96. Ludlow, *Battle of Allatoona*, 14; Grant, *Personal Memoirs*, 356.

97. *Official Records*, vol. 39, part I, 762; part II, 463.

98. Ibid., part I, 762; Raum, "With the Western Army"; Sherman, *Memoirs*, 146.

99. Hill, *From Memphis to Allatoona*, 26–32.

100. *Official Records*, vol. 39, part I, 726, 815; French, *Two Wars*, 225–26.

101. Jackson, "Holding Allatoona."

102. *Official Records*, vol. 39, part I, 815; French, *Two Wars*, 226.

103. *Official Records*, vol. 39, part I, 815; French, *Two Wars*, 226; Chambers, *Blood & Sacrifice*, 173.

104. *Official Records*, vol. 39, part I, 762–63, 773, 777, 781; *Roster and Record of Iowa Soldiers*, 945; Aldrich, *Annals of Iowa*, 291.

105. Ambrose, *History of the Seventh*, 42, 63, 142, 248.

106. *Proceedings of the Reunion Held in 1915*, 28.

107. *Official Records*, vol. 39, part I, 762; Hill, *From Memphis to Allatoona*, 32.

Chapter 9

108. Trimble, *History of the Ninety-third*, 108.

109. *Official Records*, vol. 39, part I, 785; Donahower, Towler and Kingsbury, *Glimpses of the Nation's Struggle*, 190.

110. *Official Records*, vol. 39, part I, 774, 777, 779–80, 786; Collins, "It Was a Battle." There are contradictory accounts concerning the location of the 57th Illinois. The regimental history of the 93rd Illinois places the two companies in the Eastern Redoubt. However, it gets other small details wrong later on, such as omitting movements of the 50th Illinois. The reports of Corse and Tourtellotte are completely silent on the matter. However, the regimental history of the 57th, while vague on many points, places the companies fighting with the 7th Illinois and 39th Iowa west of the railroad tracks. In addition, it specifically mentions watching the reinforcements arriving from the east side later in the battle. At no time does it mention crossing the tracks from east to west to reinforce the Star Fort. Therefore, the evidence strongly suggests that the regiment must have been somewhere on the west side to begin with.

111. *Official Records*, vol. 39, part I, 750, 751; Trimble, *History of the Ninety-third*, 108–09; *History of Green County*, 1,091; French, *Two Wars*, 226; Brown, *Battle of Allatoona*, 4–6.

112. Ludlow, *Battle of Allatoona*, 19; Trimble, *History of the Ninety-third*, 110; French, *Two Wars*, 226; *Official Records*, vol. 39, part I, 774; Brown, *History of the Fourth*, 309.

113. *Official Records*, vol. 39, part I, 750, 774, 777, 785; Ambrose, *History of the Seventh*, 253–54; Kilmer, "Allatoona Pass"; Trimble, *History of the Ninety-third*, 110, 112; Aldrich, *Annals of Iowa*, 288; Brown, *History of the Fourth*, 312.

114. French, *Two Wars*, 226, 248–49; Bevier, *History of the First and Second*, 244.

115. *Official Records*, vol. 39, part I, 816; French, *Two Wars*, 249.

116. French, *Two Wars*, 234.

117. *Official Records*, vol. 39, part I, 750, 824; Scaife, *Allatoona Pass*, 23.

118. Chambers, *Blood & Sacrifice*, 174–75.

119. *Official Records*, vol. 39, part I, 816; French, *Two Wars*, 226, 249; Trimble, *History of the Ninety-third*, 110; Scaife, *Allatoona Pass*, 23. The timing of French's surrender demand is a little vague. French himself gives two different times for when he sent Major Sanders forward with the note. In his official report, he lists 9:00 a.m. In his memoirs, he gives both 8:00 a.m. on one page, where he quotes his diary, and 9:00 a.m. later on another page. Union sources essentially give the time they received the message

as 8:30 a.m. Additionally, in all likelihood, the watches of the two officers were probably off from each other by at least thirty minutes, possibly up to an hour. Civil War timekeeping was nowhere near an exact science.

120. *Official Records*, vol. 39, part I, 763; Trimble, *History of the Ninety-third*, 110; Scaife, *Allatoona Pass*, 23; Starbuck, "Hold the Fort"; Aldrich, *Annals of Iowa*, 288.

121. Brown, *History of the Fourth*, 310–11.

122. Gottschalk, *In Deadly Earnest*, 419.

123. *Official Records*, vol. 39, part I, 763; French, *Two Wars*, 226; Starbuck, "Hold the Fort"; Gottschalk, *In Deadly Earnest*, 419; Aldrich, *Annals of Iowa*, 288.

124. Bevier, *History of the First and Second*, 244.

Chapter 10

125. *Official Records*, vol. 39, part I, 822–23; Boyce, *Captain Joseph Boyce*, 180–81; Anderson, *Memoirs*, 392; Bevier, *History of the First and Second*, 244; French, *Two Wars*, 249. The 7th Illinois and 39th Iowa had 597 between them. The 93rd had 294 on the field in ten companies. That equals about 29 men per company. Not an exact number, of course, but the best estimate that can be made under the circumstances (29 times 5 equals 145). Adding that to the 597 of the other two regiments gives the 742 in the narrative.

126. *Official Records*, vol. 39, part I, 763–64, 777; Aldrich, *Annals of Iowa*, 288; Ambrose, *History of the Seventh*, 254; *Proceedings of the Reunion Held in 1910*, 18.

127. French, *Two Wars*, 226, 249.

128. *Official Records*, vol. 39, part I, 750, 787; Trimble, *History of the Ninety-third*, 112; Bevier, *History of the First and Second*, 244–45; Boyce, *Captain Joseph Boyce*, 181; Ludlow, *Battle of Allatoona*, 36; Kilmer, "Allatoona Pass."

129. Anderson, *Memoirs*, 392; Trimble, *History of the Ninety-third*, 112–13.

130. *Official Records*, vol. 39, part I, 750; Trimble, *History of the Ninety-third*, 112; French, *Two Wars*, 249; Boyce, *Captain Joseph Boyce*, 181; Bevier, *History of the First and Second*, 245.

131. Chambers, *Blood & Sacrifice*, 175.

132. *Official Records*, vol. 39, part I, 822.

133. Ibid., 821.

134. Ibid.; Boyce, *Captain Joseph Boyce*, 181; Bradley, *Confederate Mail Carrier*, 217.

135. Aldrich, *Annals of Iowa*, 291.

136. Bevier, *History of the First and Second*, 245; Anderson, *Memoirs*, 393; Boyce, *Captain Joseph Boyce*, 181; Scaife, *Allatoona Pass*, 64.

137. Aldrich, *Annals of Iowa*, 291.

138. *Proceedings of the Reunion Held in 1910*, 18.

139. *Official Records*, vol. 39, part I, 819, 786; Aldrich, *Annals of Iowa*, 290, 293; *Roster and Record of Iowa Soldiers*, 945–46; Stroud, *Ector's Texas Brigade*, 186; Warner, *Generals in Gray*, 349.

140. Scaife, *Allatoona Pass*, 26; Boyce, *Captain Joseph Boyce*, 182; Aldrich, *Annals of Iowa*, 293.

141. *Proceedings of the Reunion Held in 1910*, 18.

142. *Official Records*, vol. 39, part I, 764, 778, 787; Trimble, *History of the Ninety-third*, 114; Donahower, Towler and Kingsbury, *Glimpses of the Nation's Struggle*, 196; Aldrich, *Annals of Iowa*, 294; The history of the 93rd Illinois claims that Captain Orrin Wilkinson, a member of that regiment and then acting as the post adjutant, carried the order from Corse to Tourtellotte. However, Flint leaves a graphic account of the journey, and Corse corroborated Flint's account in a postwar letter and mentioned him by name. It is also possible that he sent both.

143. Aldrich, *Annals of Iowa*, 290–91.

144. Trimble, *History of the Ninety-third*, 114–15; Scaife, *Allatoona Pass*, 29–30.

145. Chambers, *Blood & Sacrifice*, 175–78; Dillard letter to Mrs. Mary Clark.

146. Chambers, *Blood & Sacrifice*, 175–78.

Chapter 11

147. Brown, *History of the Fourth*, 309–10, 322, 325.

148. Ibid., 319–20.

149. *Official Records*, vol. 39, part I, 751; Brown, *History of the Fourth*, 322, 326.

150. *Official Records*, vol. 39, part I, 774, 780; Aldrich, *Annals of Iowa*, 289.

151. Chambers, *Blood & Sacrifice*, 178.

152. *Official Records*, vol. 39, part I, 749, 764; Brown, *History of the Fourth*, 312.

153. Brown, *History of the Fourth*, 315, 324–25.

154. Brown, *History of the Fourth*, 324–25; Aldrich, *Annals of Iowa*, 293.

155. Brown, *History of the Fourth*, 324–25; Aldrich, *Annals of Iowa*, 293.

156. *Official Records*, vol. 39, part I, 780; Brown, *History of the Fourth*, 323, 326; Collins, "It Was a Battle"; Aldrich, *Annals of Iowa*, 293.

157. *Official Records*, vol. 39, part I, 749, 774, 780.

158. Ibid., 780; Graham, "Colonel Hanna's Gallantry"; Hubert, *History of the Fiftieth*, 307; Cluett, *History of the 57ᵗʰ*, 82.
159. Donahower, Towler and Kingsbury, *Glimpses of the Nation's Struggle*, 196.
160. *Official Records*, vol. 39, part I, 749, 821.

CHAPTER 12

161. Ibid., 772, 781.
162. Raum, "With the Western Army." French's casualty returns confirm that one of his staff officers was captured during the battle.
163. *Official Records*, vol. 39, part I, 597, 615, 730, 741, 790; part III, 90, 95, 99.
164. Ibid., part I, 581; part III, 99; Sherman, *Memoirs*, 147.
165. *Official Records*, vol. 39, part I, 725–26; part III, 91.
166. Ibid., part I, 726; part III, 90, 92.
167. Ibid., part I, 802, 806.
168. Fish, "Signal Corps," April 26, 1883; Fish, "Signal Corps," March 1, 1888; Sherman, *Memoirs*, 147. Sherman wrote in his official report only months later that he arrived at the summit at about 10:00 a.m. Fish later recalled that it was "just after daybreak," which would have been considerably earlier, and Sherman in his memoirs contradicts his own report and says that it was about 8:00 a.m.
169. *Official Records*, vol. 39, part III, 96–97; Fish, "On Kenesaw's Top"; Sherman, *Memoirs*, 147.
170. *Official Records*, vol. 39, part I, 740; Brown, *History of the Fourth*, 320–21.
171. *Official Records*, vol. 39, part I, 816; part III, 100.

CHAPTER 13

172. *Official Records*, vol. 39, part I, 821, 823; Yeary, ed., *Reminiscences*, 617.
173. *Official Records*, vol. 39, part I, 780; Trimble, *History of the Ninety-third*, 116, 118; Donahower, Towler and Kingsbury, *Glimpses of the Nation's Struggle*, 197; Ludlow, *Battle of Allatoona*, 32; Collins, "It Was a Battle"; Graham, "Colonel Hanna's Gallantry."

174. *Official Records*, vol. 39, part I, 751, 818, 825; Brown, *History of the Fourth*, 312, 324.

175. Brown, *History of the Fourth*, 323.

176. Ibid., 322.

177. Aldrich, *Annals of Iowa*, 288.

178. Trimble, *History of the Ninety-third*, 117–18; Whitney, "Allatoona."

179. Ambrose, *History of the Seventh*, 267–68; Hallet, "12th Ill. at Allatoona."

180. *Official Records*, vol. 39, part I, 542, 725–26, 790, 816; part III, 100.

181. Ibid., part I, 781; Ludlow, *Battle of Allatoona*, 32; Donahower, Towler and Kingsbury, *Glimpses of the Nation's Struggle*, 197; Hubert, *History of the Fiftieth*, 307.

182. *Official Records*, vol. 39, part I, 765; Donahower, Towler and Kingsbury, *Glimpses of the Nation's Struggle*, 198–99; Ludlow, *Battle of Allatoona*, 32–33. Pictures taken of Corse after his subsequent promotion to major general show no sign of any permanent injury or scarring on either his cheek or ear, left or right. However, the impact could have still knocked him senseless as described.

183. Trimble, *History of the Ninety-third*, 119.

184. *Official Records*, vol. 39, part I, 765; Donahower, Towler and Kingsbury, *Glimpses of the Nation's Struggle*, 200; Ludlow, *Battle of Allatoona*, 32; Aldrich, *Annals of Iowa*, 290; Trimble, *History of the Ninety-third*, 119; Raum, "With the Western Army."

185. *Official Records*, vol. 39, part I, 765, 816; Kibbe, "Allatoona"; Anderson, *Memoirs*, 393; French, *Two Wars*, 255; Boyce, *Captain Joseph Boyce*, 182; Brown, *Battle of Allatoona*, 8.

186. *Official Records*, vol. 39, part I, 765; Brown, *History of the Fourth*, 311; Cluett, *History of the 57th*, 82; Aldrich, *Annals of Iowa*, 292–93.

187. Brown, *History of the Fourth*, 323; Ludlow, *Battle of Allatoona*, 33.

188. *Official Records*, vol. 39, part I, 816–17; French, *Two Wars*, 255–56.

189. French, *Two Wars*, 256; Bevier, *History of the First and Second*, 246.

CHAPTER 14

190. *Official Records*, vol. 39, part I, 817; French, *Two Wars*, 256; Landry, diary.

191. French, *Two Wars*, 256; Brown, *Battle of Allatoona*, 12.

192. Chambers, *Blood & Sacrifice*, 178–79.

193. Dillard, letter to Mrs. Mary Clark.

194. Trimble, *History of the Ninety-third*, 119; Starbuck, "Hold the Fort."

195. Brown, *History of the Fourth*, 312; Aldrich, *Annals of Iowa*, 291; Trimble, *History of the Ninety-third*, 119–20.

196. *Official Records*, vol. 39, part I, 751; Brown, *History of the Fourth*, 324.

197. *Official Records*, vol. 39, part I, 817; French, *Two Wars*, 256–57; Yeary, *Reminiscences*, 617; Bevier, *History of the First and Second*, 246.

198. Chambers, *Blood & Sacrifice*, 179.

199. Dillard, letter to Mrs. Mary Clark; Dillard, letter to Mrs. W.H. Clark. Clark's slave rode the colonel's horse through Union lines, traveling from Georgia to Mississippi, and delivered the colonel's personal belongings to his family. After the war, the colonel's body was recovered and reburied in Brandon, Mississippi.

200. *Official Records*, vol. 39, part I, 817, 822; French, *Two Wars*, 234.

201. *Official Records*, vol. 39, part III, 96–97; Hubert, *History of the Fiftieth*, 308; Fish, "Signal Corps," April 26, 1883.

202. *Official Records*, vol. 39, part I, 751–52, 817–18.

203. Boyce, *Captain Joseph Boyce*, 182–83; Chapman, *Roster of Wisconsin Volunteers*, 83–111. Accounts vary on the number of men surrendered at the blockhouse. Lieutenant Colonel Jackson in his report submitted a list that noted four officers and seventy-seven enlisted men capture for the regiment for entire battle. A careful examination of the report of the Wisconsin adjutant general lists eighty-two men captured in Companies E, F and I at Allatoona. I went with the adjutant general's report. Also, there is no listing for a Captain O'Brien on the 18th Wisconsin's roster, although Captain Carpenter did exist. The simplest explanation is that Boyce just remembered the name incorrectly.

204. French, *Two Wars*, 285.

Chapter 15

205. Trimble, *History of the Ninety-third*, 119.

206. Ibid., 120.

207. Collins, "It Was a Battle."

208. Aldrich, *Annals of Iowa*, 292.

209. *Proceedings of the Reunion Held in 1910*, 18.

210. *Official Records*, vol. 39, part I, 762; Ludlow, *Battle of Allatoona*, 31; Brown, *History of the Fourth*, 323.

211. *Official Records*, vol. 39, part I, 781; Aldrich, *Annals of Iowa*, 288; Raum, "With the Western Army."

212. *Official Records*, vol. 39, part III, 97.

213. Ibid., part I, 597–98, 725–26, 730, 790; part III, 92–94.

214. Hubert, *History of the Fiftieth*, 309; Trimble, *History of the Ninety-third*, 131.

215. *Official Records*, vol. 39, part I, 766, 785; Livermore, *Numbers and Losses*, 79, 97, 102.

216. *Official Records*, vol. 39, part I, 766, 818–20; French, *Two Wars*, 263; Brown, *Battle of Allatoona*, 16. Upon reaching the safety of New Hope Church on the morning of October 6, the wounded General Young insisted on continuing south to Newnan. Despite being warned about the Federal cavalry nearby, he left shortly thereafter. He was captured within three hours by Garrard's cavalrymen.

217. *Official Records*, vol. 39, part I, 773; Trimble, *History of the Ninety-third*, 131; Brown, *History of the Fourth*, 323.

218. *Official Records*, vol. 39, part III, 113–14; Fish, "Signal Corps," April 26, 1883.

219. *Official Records*, vol. 39, part I, 806; part III, 114; Trimble, *History of the Ninety-third*, 132; Cox, *Atlanta*, 233.

220. Sherman, *Memoirs*, 150.

221. Foote, *Civil War*, 612. It's a nice story, but Foote failed to provide any sources in his narrative. Also, Sherman makes no mention of it in his memoirs. There is a good chance that this encounter is apocryphal.

222. *Official Records*, vol. 39, part I, 807; Sherman, *Memoirs*, 167.

223. *Official Records*, vol. 39, part III, 324; Sherman, *Memoirs*, 151, 157.

Appendix B

224. Kurtz, Notebook 20, 140.

ORDER OF BATTLE

225. *Official Records*, vol. 39, part I, 762; Chapman, *Roster of Wisconsin Volunteers*, 83–111. This strength is derived from adding the 150 men listed in Colonel Jackson's official report, plus an estimated 12 officers, and finally adding in the 82 men captured at the blockhouse.

226. *Official Records*, vol. 39, part I, 750.

227. Ibid., 748, 762. An estimated 22 officers were added to the 450 "guns" listed in the regiment's official report.

228. Ibid., 748.

229. Trimble, *History of the Ninety-third*, 101.

230. *Official Records*, vol. 39, part I, 773.

231. Ibid., 777. The official report for the regiment lists 291 muskets and 8 musicians, to which I added an estimated 14 officers.

232. Ibid., 781.

233. Ibid., 763. Sixty-one men listed in the regiment's official report, adding in an estimated five officers.

234. Ibid., 785.

235. Ibid., part II, 838. The last formal report of the division's strength was on September 20, 1864. The number in parentheses, 2,250, represents an estimate of those men actually engaged in the assault. It does not include teamsters, artillery, the 4th Mississippi (left behind to invest the blockhouse) or the 32nd Texas Cavalry and 39th North Carolina (left at Moore's Hill to guard the artillery).

236. Ibid., part I, 818; French, *Two Wars*, 249. General Young was captured the day after the battle and so did not leave a report. The strength of the four regiments that participated in the assault was four hundred, according to French, and this does not include the 32nd Texas Cavalry and 39th North Carolina. The brigade's casualties were listed in French's official report.

237. *Official Records*, vol. 39, part I, 824. The regimental report lists "eighty-seven guns," to which an estimated five officers were added.

238. Ibid., 823.

239. Ibid., 821.

240. Ibid., 822. The regiment reported two men wounded while skirmishing south of the pass.

241. Ibid., 820; French, letter, 1866. In his letter written in 1866, French lists the strength of Cockrell's Brigade as 1,050, including calculations based on casualties and the strength of the unit at Franklin two months later.

However, in his biography, French revised it to 950. I chose to use the larger number because it was written closer to the end of the war and was derived from solid calculations of casualties and strengths. An addendum to French's report breaks down the casualties of the brigade by regiment.

242. *Official Records*, vol. 39, part I, 818, 820. An estimate, based on French stating that he assaulted with little more than two thousand men. An addendum to French's report breaks down the casualties of the brigade by regiment.

243. Ibid., vol. 38, part III, 683. An estimate based on the strength of Myrick's Battalion in a report dated September 20, 1864.

Bibliography

Aldrich, Charles A.M., ed. *The Annals of Iowa: A Historical Quarterly*. Vol. 2, 3rd series. Des Moines: Historical Department of Iowa, 1895–97.

Ambrose, D. Leib. *History of the Seventh Regiment Illinois Volunteer Infantry, from Its First Muster into the U.S. Service, April 25, 1861, to Its Final Muster Out, July 9 1865*. Springfield: Illinois Journal Company, 1868.

Anderson, Ephraim McD. *Memoirs: Historical and Personal; Including the Campaigns of the First Missouri Brigade*. St. Louis, MO: Times Printing Company, 1868.

Barber, Lucius W. *Army Memoirs of Lucius W. Barber, Company "D" 15th Illinois Volunteer Infantry*. Chicago, IL: J.M.W. Jones Stationery and Printing Company, 1894.

Bevier, R.S. *History of the First and Second Missouri Confederate Brigades, 1861–1865*. St. Louis, MO: Bryan, Brand & Company, 1879.

Boyce, Joseph. *Captain Joseph Boyce and the 1st Missouri Infantry, C.S.A.* Edited by William C. Winter. St. Louis: University of Missouri Press, 2011.

Bradley, James. *The Confederate Mail Carrier, or From Missouri to Arkansas, Through Mississippi, Alabama, Georgia and Tennessee*. Mexico, MO, 1894.

Brown, Alonzo L. *History of the Fourth Regiment of Minnesota Infantry Volunteers During the Great Rebellion 1861–1865*. St. Paul, MN: Pioneer Press Company, 1892.

Brown, Joseph M. *The Battle of Allatoona, October 5, 1864*. Atlanta, GA: Record Publishing Company, 1890.

Castel, Albert. *Decision in the West: The Atlanta Campaign of 1864*. Lawrence: University Press of Kansas, 1992.

Chambers, William Pitt. *Blood & Sacrifice: The Journal of a Confederate Soldier*. Edited by Richard A. Baumgartner. Huntington, WV: Blue Acorn Press, 1994.

Chapman, Chandler P., ed. *Roster of Wisconsin Volunteers, War of the Rebellion, 1861–1865*. Vol. 2. Madison, WI: Democrat Printing Company, 1886.

Cluett, William W. *History of the 57th Regiment Illinois Volunteer Infantry, from Muster in, Dec. 26, 1861, to Muster Out, July 7, 1865*. Princeton, CT: T.P. Streeter, Printer, 1886.

Collins, L.R. "It Was a Battle." *National Tribune*, October 11, 1883.

Cox, Jacob D. *Atlanta*. New York: Charles Scribner's Sons, 1882.

Davis, Jefferson. *The Rise and Fall of the Confederate Government*. Vol. 2. New York: D. Appleton and Company, 1881.

Davis, Oliver Wilson. *Life of David Bell Birney, Major-General United States Volunteers*. Philadelphia: King & Baird, 1867.

Dillard, G.G. Letter to Mrs. Mary Clark, undated. In possession of Susan Fernie, Beaumont, Texas.

———. Letter to Mrs. W.H. Clark, October 8, 1864. In possession of Susan Fernie, Beaumont, Texas.

Donahower, J.C., Silas H. Towler and David L. Kingsbury. *Glimpses of the Nation's Struggle*. 5th Series. St. Paul, MN: Review Publishing Company, 1908.

Ecelbarger, Gary. *The Day Dixie Died: The Battle of Atlanta*. New York: Thomas Dunne Books, 2010.

Etowah Valley Historical Society. "The Unknown Hero of Allatoona Pass." Cartersville, GA: Etowah Valley Historical Society, n.d.

Evans, David. *Sherman's Horsemen: Union Cavalry Operations in the Atlanta Campaign*. Bloomington: Indiana University Press, 1996.

Fish, C.H. "On Kenesaw's Top." *National Tribune*, August 6, 1896.

———. "The Signal Corps." *National Tribune*, April 19, 1883.

———. "The Signal Corps." *National Tribune*, April 26, 1883.

———. "The Signal Corps." *National Tribune*, March 1, 1888.

Flatau, L.S. "Only Regiment of Confederate Artillery." *Confederate Veteran* 15, no. 9 (September 1907): 410.

Foote, Shelby. *The Civil War, a Narrative: Red River to Appomattox*. New York: Random House, 1974.

Foster, Samuel T. *One of Cleburne's Command: The Civil War Reminiscences and Diary of Capt. Samuel T. Foster, Granbury's Brigade, CSA*. Edited by Norman D. Brown. Austin: University of Texas Press, 1980.

Frankenberry, A. D. "Visiting War Scenes." *National Tribune*, January 16, 1896.

French, Samuel G. Letter, May 3, 1866. MSS 840, Box 1, Folder 7. James L. Mitchell Collection, Atlanta Historical Center, Atlanta, Georgia.

————. *Two Wars: An Autobiography of Gen. Samuel G. French, an Officer in the Army of the United States and the Confederate States, a Graduate from the U.S. Military Academy, West Point, 1843.* Nashville, TN: Confederate Veteran, 1901.

Gottschalk, Phil. *In Deadly Earnest: The Missouri Brigade.* Columbia: Missouri River Press, 1991.

Graham, J.D. "Colonel Hanna's Gallantry." *National Tribune,* October 11, 1883.

Grant, U.S. *Personal Memoirs of U.S. Grant.* Vol. 2. New York: Charles L. Webster & Company, 1885.

Hallet, W.H. "The 12th Ill. at Allatoona." *National Tribune,* June 4, 1908.

Hill, George W. *From Memphis to Allatoona, and the Battle of Allatoona, October 5, 1864.* Providence, RI: Providence Press, 1891.

History of Green County, Wisconsin. Springfield, IL: Union Publishing Company, 1884.

Hood, J.B. *Advance and Retreat: Personal Experiences in the United States and Confederate States Armies.* Philadelphia: Burk & M'Fetridge, 1880.

Hubert, Charles F. *History of the Fiftieth Regiment Illinois Volunteer Infantry in the War of the Union.* Kansas City, MO: Western Veteran Publishing Company, 1894.

Jackson, Thos. A. "Holding Allatoona." *National Tribune,* January 3, 1884.

Jones, J. William, ed. *Southern Historical Society Papers.* Vol. 10. Richmond, VA: William Ellis Jones, 1882.

Kibbe, A.R. "Allatoona." *National Tribune,* October 30, 1884.

Kilmer, George L. "Allatoona Pass." *Yakima Herald,* August 3, 1893.

Kirk, Charles H. *History of the Fifteenth Pennsylvania Volunteer Cavalry Which Was Recruited and Known as the Anderson Cavalry in the Rebellion of 1861–1865.* Philadelphia, 1906.

Kurtz, Wilbur. Notebook 20. MSS 130, Box 3.270. Atlanta History Center, Atlanta, Georgia.

Landry, Caesar. Diary transcription. Included in M-089, Evander McNair Graham Family, Papers, 1812–1965, Box 004, Folder 005. Special Collections, Manuscripts and Archives, Prescott Memorial Library, Louisiana Tech University, Ruston, Louisiana.

Laraba, John. "Graced the Captain's Table." *National Tribune,* September 23, 1897.

Livermore, Thomas L. *Numbers and Losses in the Civil War in America 1861–65.* Boston: Houghton, Mifflin and Company, 1900.

Lowry, Horace S. "Taken in at Big Shanty." *National Tribune*, September 23, 1897.

Ludlow, William. *The Battle of Allatoona, October 5th 1864: A Paper Read Before the Michigan Commandery of the Military Order of the Loyal Legion of the U.S.* Detroit, MI: Winn & Hammond, Printers and Binders, 1891.

Nanzig, Thomas P., ed. *The Badax Tigers: From Shiloh to the Surrender with the 18th Wisconsin Volunteers.* Lanham, MD: Rowman & Littlefield Publishers Inc., 2008.

Newton, Steven H. *Lost for the Cause: The Confederate Army in 1864.* Mason City, IA: Savas Publishing Company, 2000.

Patrick, Robert. *Reluctant Rebel: The Secret Diary of Robert Patrick, 1861–1865.* Edited by F. Jay Taylor. Baton Rouge: Louisiana State University Press, 1959.

Porter, Horace. *Campaigning with Grant.* New York: Century Company, 1907.

Powell, David A. *The Maps of Chickamauga.* New York: Savas Beatte, 2009.

Proceedings of the Reunion Held in 1915 by the Association of Survivors Seventh Regiment Illinois Veteran Infantry Volunteers at Springfield, Illinois. Springfield, IL: State Register Printing House, 1915.

Proceedings of the Reunion Held in 1910 by the Association of Survivors Seventh Regiment Illinois Veteran Infantry Volunteers at Springfield, Illinois. Springfield, IL: State Register Printing House, 1911.

Raines, Rebecca Robins. *Getting the Message Through: A Branch History of the U.S. Army Signal Corps.* Washington, D.C.: U.S. Government Printing Office, 2011.

Raum, Green B. "With the Western Army." *National Tribune*, January 22 and 29, 1903.

Roster and Record of Iowa Soldiers in the War of the Rebellion Together with Historical Sketches of Volunteer Organizations 1861–1865. Vol. 5. Des Moines, IA: Emory H. English, State Printer, 1911.

Scaife, William R. *Allatoona Pass: A Needless Effusion of Blood.* Cartersville, GA: Etowah Valley Historical Society, 1995.

Sherman, W.T. *Personal Memoirs of Gen. W.T. Sherman.* Vol. 2. New York: Charles L. Webster & Company, 1890.

Starbuck, E. "Hold the Fort." *National Tribune*, October 1, 1903.

Stroud, David V. *Ector's Texas Brigade and the Army of Tennessee, 1862–1865.* Longview, TX: Ranger Publishing, 2004.

Sword, Wiley. *The Confederacy's Last Hurrah: Spring Hill, Franklin & Nashville.* Lawrence: University Press of Kansas, 1992.

Trimble, Harvey M. *History of the Ninety-third Regiment Illinois Volunteer Infantry from Organization to Muster Out.* Chicago, IL: Blakely Printing Company, 1898.

U.S. War Department. *The War of the Rebellion: A Compilation of the Official Records of the Union and Confederate Armies*. 128 vols. Washington, D.C.: Government Printing Office, 1880–1901.

Warner, Ezra J. *Generals in Blue: Lives of the Union Commanders*. Baton Rouge: Louisiana State University Press, 1964.

————. *Generals in Gray: Lives of the Confederate Commanders*. Baton Rouge: Louisiana State University Press, 2000.

Wheeler's Confederate Cavalry Association. *Campaigns of Wheeler and His Cavalry 1862–1865*. Edited by W.C. Dodson. Atlanta, GA: Hudgins Publishing Company, 1899.

Whitney, J.J. "Allatoona." *National Tribune*, August 28, 1884.

Woodworth, Steven W. *Nothing but Victory: The Army of the Tennessee 1861–1865*. New York: Alfred A. Knopf, 2005.

Wright, Henry H. *A History of the Sixth Iowa Infantry*. Iowa City: State Historical Society of Iowa, 1923.

Yeary, Maime, ed. *Reminiscences of the Boys in Gray 1861–1865*. Dallas, TX: Smith & Lamar Publishing House, 1912.

Index

Rich, Wilson W. 122
Ritchy, Henry 111
Rogers, George 110
Rogers, George C. 64
Rome, Georgia 29, 40, 45, 65, 69,
    81, 115, 145, 146
Rowett, Richard 81, 87, 91, 96, 98,
    103, 128, 142
Rowett's Redoubt 103, 142, 147
Ruff's Station, Georgia 67
Russell, Edward U. 135
Russell, Isaac 110

S

Sanders, David W. 90
Savannah, Georgia 22, 29, 36, 45,
    46
Savidge, Charles H. 112
Schofield, John M. 28, 44
Sears' Brigade 136
Sears, Claudius W. 34, 35, 89, 96,
    122, 133
Selma, Alabama 29
Sherman, William Tecumseh 21,
    22, 27, 39, 50, 62, 65, 81, 116,
    131, 143, 145
Shiloh, Battle of 32, 53, 81, 144
Signal Mountain 90
Smith, Augustus 140
Smith, John A. 82, 96, 101, 142
Smith, John E. 40, 46, 142
Smyrna Camp Ground, Georgia 66,
    116
Stanley, David S. 40, 66, 69
Starbuck, Elisha 91, 134
Star Fort 52, 81, 85, 86, 96, 102,
    108, 109, 112, 120, 130, 141,
    145
Stewart, Alexander P. 23, 67, 117
Stone's River, Battle of 22, 33, 34,
    144
Sweeney, Thomas W. 28, 73

T

Tennessee Road 49, 108, 122
Thomas, George H. 27, 40, 44, 45
Tourtellotte, John E. 55, 56, 65, 70,
    75, 88, 102, 107, 108, 112,
    122, 123, 142
Towle, Daniel G. 86, 90
Trimble, Harvey M. 96, 121, 134, 141

U

Union units
    4th Minnesota Infantry 51, 53, 86,
        92, 96, 107, 114, 119, 144, 145
    4th U.S. Cavalry 126
    5th Ohio Cavalry 53
    6th Iowa Infantry 73, 74
    7th Illinois Infantry 81, 95, 103,
        124, 144, 147
    7th Iowa Infantry 115
    12th Illinois Infantry 81, 85, 107,
        124
    12th Wisconsin Battery 53, 86, 87,
        107, 129, 142
    14th and 15th Illinois Infantry
        Battalion 63, 126
    18th Wisconsin Infantry 53, 79, 86,
        87, 107, 114, 122
    32nd Illinois Infantry 126
    39th Iowa Infantry 33, 81, 86, 95,
        99, 134, 144
    41st Illinois Infantry 126
    50th Illinois Infantry 81, 85, 102,
        107, 122, 126
    52nd Illinois Infantry 115
    57th Illinois Infantry 81, 85, 86, 87,
        115
    93rd Illinois Infantry 53, 57, 86, 91,
        101, 103, 127, 145
    Army of the Cumberland 27, 40,
        42, 62, 66, 116, 125
    Army of the Ohio 28, 44, 69, 116,
        120, 125

About the Author

Brad Butkovich has a Bachelor of Arts degree in history from Georgia Southern University. He spent more than a decade in the role-playing game publishing industry, took time off to be a stay-at-home parent and is now head of customer service at a major corporation. He is a member of the Northeast Georgia Civil War Round Table. He has published several books on American Civil War miniature gaming and recently published a book on the Battle of Pickett's Mill. He has always had a keen interest in Civil War history, photography and cartography, all of which have come together in his current projects.